Windows™
QuickStart,
3.11 Edition

Ron Person
and Laura Acklen

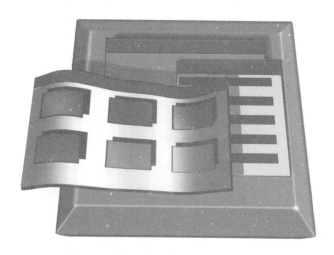

Windows QuickStart, 3.11 Edition

Copyright © 1994 by Que® Corporation.

Library of Congress Catalog No.: 94-67368

ISBN: 1-56529-865-9

96 95 94   4 3 2 1

Interpretation of the printing code: the rightmost double-digit number is the year of the book's printing; the rightmost single-digit number is the number of the book's printing. For example, a printing code of 94-1 shows that the first printing of the book occurred in 1994.

Screens reproduced in this book were created using Collage Complete from Inner Media, Inc., Hollis, NH.

Publisher: David P. Ewing

Associate Publisher: Michael Miller

Publishing Director: Joseph B. Wikert

Managing Editor: Michael Cunningham

Product Marketing Manager: Greg Wiegand

Dedication

To Jeff, a wonderful husband and father. I am very lucky to have you in my life.

Laura Acklen

About the Authors

Ron Person has written more than 12 books for Que Corporation, including *Using Excel 5 for Windows*, Special Edition, and *Using Word 6 for Windows*, Special Edition. Ron is the principal consultant for Ron Person & Co. He has an M.S. in physics from the Ohio State University and an M.B.A. from Hardin-Simmons University.

Ron Person & Co., based in San Francisco, has attained Microsoft's highest rating for Microsoft Excel and Word for Windows consultants—Microsoft Solutions Partner. Ron was one of Microsoft's 12 original Consulting Partners. The firm trains Excel and Visual Basic for Applications developers and support staff for corporations nationally and internationally. If your company plans to develop applications using Microsoft Excel or integrating multiple Microsoft applications, you will gain significantly from the courses taught by Ron Person & Co. For information on course content, on-site corporate classes, or consulting, contact Ron Person & Co. at the following address:

> Ron Person & Co.
> P.O. Box 5647
> Santa Rosa, CA 95402

Laura Acklen is an independent author and instructor located in Austin, Texas. She has been training and supporting computer users in DOS and Windows products since 1986. Laura has written over 15 student manuals and instructor guides for the national training company Productivity Point International. She is the author of Que's *WordPerfect 6.0 SureSteps* and coauthor of *Oops! WordPerfect: What To Do When Things Go Wrong*. She is also a contributing author of *Using WordPerfect Version 6 for Windows*, Special Edition.

Publishing Manager
Brad R. Koch

Acquisitions Editor
Angela J. Lee

Product Directors
Robin Drake
C. Kazim Haidri

Production Editor
Virginia Noble

Editors
Lori L. Cates
Lynn Northrup
Maureen Schneeberger
Kathy Simpson

Technical Editor
Kurt Barthelmess

Book Designer
Amy Peppler-Adams

Cover Designer
Sandra Stevenson

Production Team
Stephen Adams
Angela Bannan
Stephen Carlin
Karen Dodson
Chad Dressler
DiMonique Ford
Malinda Lowder
Wendy Ott
G. Alan Palmore
Caroline Roop
Clair Schweinler
Michael Thomas

Indexer
Charlotte Clapp

Acquisitions Coordinator
Patricia J. Brooks

Editorial Assistant
Michelle Williams

Composed in *Stone Serif* and *MCPdigital* by Que Corporation.

Acknowledgments

I have thoroughly enjoyed working with everyone on the production team for this *QuickStart* book. This book has truly been a group effort, and I want to take the opportunity to thank all those involved.

I would like to gratefully acknowledge the assistance I received from my Acquisitions Editor, Angie Lee. She not only coordinated the entire project schedule but also kept me motivated and on schedule, despite the increasing scope of the project. Thanks also to Patty Brooks, Acquisitions Coordinator, for obtaining all the necessary products and equipment.

Thanks to Brad Koch, Publishing Manager, for his assistance in developing the outline for the book. I would like to thank Chris Haidri, Product Director, for his help in the critical early stages of the project. I owe a very special thanks to Robin Drake, Product Director. She cheerfully switched gears at a moment's notice for brainstorming sessions and "took the ball and ran with it" during editing. Most of all, I thank Robin for her depth of experience that made this book as practical and realistic as possible.

I would also like to acknowledge the fine job done by Ginny Noble, Production Editor. Ginny's tireless attention to detail and thoughtful questions contributed to the accuracy and clarity of the manuscript.

Last, but not least, thanks to Kurt Barthelmess for his painstaking technical review. His suggestions made a significant contribution to the book. Thanks also to Michael Watson for his assistance in the final review of the Workgroups chapters.

Laura Acklen

Trademark Acknowledgments

All terms mentioned in this book that are known to be trademarks or service marks have been appropriately capitalized. Que cannot attest to the accuracy of this information. Use of a term in this book should not be regarded as affecting the validity of any trademark or service mark.

We'd Like to Hear from You!

As part of our continuing effort to produce books of the highest possible quality, Que would like to hear your comments. To stay competitive, we *really* want you, as a computer book reader and user, to let us know what you like or dislike most about this book or other Que products.

You can mail comments, ideas, or suggestions for improving future editions to the address provided here, or send us a fax at (317) 581-4663. For the on-line inclined, Macmillan Computer Publishing now has a forum on CompuServe (type **go quebooks** at any prompt) through which our staff and authors are available for questions and comments. In addition to exploring our forum, please feel free to contact me personally on CompuServe at 72002,2515 to discuss your opinions of this book.

Thanks in advance—your comments will help us to continue publishing the best books available on computer topics in today's market.

Robin Drake
Product Development Specialist
Que Corporation
201 W. 103rd Street
Indianapolis, Indiana 46290
USA

Contents at a Glance

Table of Contents

Introduction

Welcome to *Windows QuickStart*, 3.11 Edition. Whether you are a novice with computers or are familiar with DOS programs, this *QuickStart* provides one of the easiest and fastest ways to join the Windows revolution.

You will find that Windows 3.11 makes personal computers more accessible, even to first-time computer users, and moves you further up the productivity curve. Controlled studies, surveys, and the experience of thousands of students have shown that Windows programs help new users learn more quickly and help experienced users become more productive. Aside from increasing your productivity, Windows and Windows programs are more fun to use than character-based DOS programs.

Windows 3.11 for Workgroups is the latest release of an exciting new product that brings the features of local area networks to Windows. Workgroup management features enable you to share information and network resources (such as files and printers) with your coworkers. The electronic mail and workgroup scheduling programs have been enhanced with the latest release, and a PC Fax program has been added to enable you to send faxes from Mail or from a Windows application.

Who Should Use This Book?

The *QuickStart* series is designed for adult, self-paced learning. You might consider *Windows QuickStart*, 3.11 Edition, your own personal instructor. The book presents enough basic information to get a first-time user started and then builds on that user's growing understanding by introducing more advanced topics. Because the lessons are modular in design, you can work straight through the book, or you can select only those lessons that contain features you want to know more about.

What you learn in *Windows QuickStart*, 3.11 Edition, carries over to Windows programs, such as Microsoft Excel and Microsoft Word for Windows, because all Windows programs work in a similar way. After you learn the basics, you're well on your way to understanding any new Windows program.

If you are an experienced personal computer user but are not familiar with Windows, you will find *Windows QuickStart*, 3.11 Edition, an excellent way to come up to speed quickly. When you need more detailed information, you can turn to Que's *Using Windows*, 3.11 Edition, Special Edition.

In addition, *Windows QuickStart*, 3.11 Edition, provides details on Windows 3.11 for Workgroups for those readers who use the Workgroups version—probably on a network. Information specific to Windows for Workgroups is marked with a special icon in the margin.

How This Book Is Organized

Each lesson begins with a brief introduction and a bulleted list of topics covered. Lessons are organized into a series of tasks, which are step-by-step instructions for completing specific functions. Within the tasks are notes that provide additional information, and cautions that warn you about potential difficulty. There are also problem-solving paragraphs that help get you out of trouble. Each lesson ends with an "On Your Own" section, containing exercises for testing what you learned in the lesson.

This book is divided into four parts, as described in the following sections.

Part I: Getting Started with Windows

The lessons in Part I provide basic information about Windows. Review these lessons if you have never used Windows or if you need to review the Windows environment.

Lesson 1, "Learning the Basics," shows you how to start and exit Windows. You learn about the parts of the Program Manager window, how to use the mouse, how to use menus and dialog boxes, and how to use the Help system.

Lesson 2, "Working with Windows," takes you through the process of minimizing, maximizing, and restoring windows. You learn how to resize and move windows and how to view multiple group windows.

Part II: Customizing Windows

In this part of the book, you learn how to organize and run your programs in Windows. These lessons cover customizing your Windows working environment and controlling printers and fonts.

Lesson 3, "Working with Groups and Applications," teaches you how to arrange your program icons in group windows. You learn how to add and remove groups and programs, how to change the setup, and how to move and copy icons between group windows.

Lesson 4, "Starting and Controlling Applications," shows you how to start your applications. You use the Task List to switch between open applications and to display multiple application windows at once. You learn also how to access the DOS prompt from Windows.

Lesson 5, "Personalizing Windows," shows you how to customize your working environment. You change screen colors and select desktop patterns, wallpaper, and screen savers. You learn how to change the system date and time, change the icon spacing, enable fast switching, and fine-tune the mouse response. Finally, you learn how to assign sounds to system events and turn sounds on and off.

Lesson 6, "Controlling Printers and Fonts," shows you how to use Print Manager to manage print jobs on a local printer and on a network printer. In addition, you learn how to work with the Windows TrueType fonts.

Part III: Managing Files with File Manager

Part III explores the use of File Manager to manage your files, directories, and disks. The last lesson in this section discusses working with network drives.

Lesson 7, "Displaying and Organizing Files," helps you manage your files. You learn how to use File Manager to view the contents of a directory on any drive available on your system. You can open multiple directory windows and arrange them on-screen. This lesson describes how to search for files and sort the file list. You learn how to create file associations and how to start programs from File Manager. Finally, you learn how to use the special File Manager toolbar for Windows for Workgroups users.

Lesson 8, "Managing Files, Directories, and Disks," shows you how to select, move, copy, rename, and delete files and directories. You learn how to format and copy floppy disks. The MS-DOS tools that can be integrated into File Manager are identified and discussed.

Lesson 9, "Working with Network Drives," teaches you how to work with shared directories on a network. Note that this lesson applies primarily to Windows for Workgroups users.

Part IV: Working with Windows Applications

Part IV begins by showing you how to use the Write word processing program provided with Windows. The experience you gain with Write is applicable to most other Windows word processing programs. For Workgroups users, this part of the book provides lessons on using the electronic mail, personal fax, and workgroup scheduler programs. These lessons also show you how to install and configure DOS applications and how to share data between applications.

Lesson 10, "Using Write," shows you how to use the word processing program included with Windows. You learn how to create, edit, print, and save documents. You learn also how to open existing files (for example, the WRI files that come with Windows to provide additional documentation) and how to enhance your text.

Lesson 11, "Using Mail and PC Fax," teaches you how to use the Mail and PC Fax programs included with Windows for Workgroups. You learn how to send messages to your coworkers and how to read, reply, forward, print, and delete your own messages. You learn how to attach a file to a mail message and organize your messages into mail folders. PC Fax is used to send faxes from within Windows programs or from Mail. You learn how to send, receive, and print faxes.

Lesson 12, "Using Schedule+," shows you how to use the Schedule+ program to schedule meetings, thereby saving effort when trying to arrange a mutually agreeable date and time. You learn how to respond to meeting requests from your coworkers, read responses to your meeting requests, and reschedule and cancel meetings.

Lesson 13, "Installing and Configuring DOS Applications," provides you with the steps for starting DOS programs from Program Manager and File Manager. You learn how to create and edit program information files (PIF files). You learn also how to switch between running a DOS program full-screen and running the program in a window, as well as how to switch between DOS programs.

Lesson 14, "Sharing Data between Applications," teaches you how to share data between applications. You learn how to use the Windows Clipboard to copy and link data. You learn also about the Windows Dynamic Data Exchange (DDE) and Object Linking and Embedding (OLE) concepts.

Appendixes

Appendix A, "Installing Windows 3.11 or Windows for Workgroups 3.11," guides you through the basics of the Windows Setup program. This section also includes the system requirements needed to run Windows 3.11 or Windows for Workgroups 3.11.

Appendix B, "Optimizing Windows 3.11," provides information on what you can do to improve Windows performance on your system.

How to Use This Book

If you like, you can work through this book sequentially, reading one lesson at a time and learning as you go. If you have special needs, you can go directly to the lessons that provide the information. Each lesson is independent, so you can approach the book in any order.

If You	Turn To
Have no experience with Windows	Lessons 1–2
Want to learn how to minimize and maximize windows	Lesson 2
Want to learn how to start applications	Lesson 4
Want to customize Windows	Lesson 5
Want to manage your files	Lessons 7–8
Want to use the Mail or PC Fax program	Lesson 11

(continues)

If You	Turn To
Need to schedule a meeting	Lesson 12
Need to start and control DOS programs	Lesson 13
Need to copy data between programs in Windows	Lesson 14

Throughout this book are several elements designed to make the book easier to use. Notes in text provide additional useful information. *If you have problems...* paragraphs help you troubleshoot potential problems. In the margin are key terms and cautions. Key terms are defined terms used in Windows, and cautions are just that—items that caution you about a potential problem or error.

Where to Find More Help

After you master the information in this book, you may want to learn more about Windows, DOS, and Windows-based application programs. Que publishes a range of books that may be helpful. The *Using* series provides detailed information for intermediate and advanced users, covering all major features of the program. *Using Windows*, 3.11 Edition, Special Edition, contains up-to-date coverage of Windows and Windows for Workgroups. If you want a handy reference to the major Windows functions and commands that you can keep near the computer, consider *Windows VisiRef* (a visual reference). If you are working with Windows for Workgroups, you may want to consult Que's *Connecting Windows for Workgroups 3.1*.

Windows 3.11 also provides extensive on-line help to answer many of your questions. To learn how to access Windows Help, see Lesson 1, "Learning the Basics."

Conventions Used in This Book

Windows QuickStart, 3.11 Edition, follows certain conventions to help you understand the information in the book:

- Text that you are instructed to type appears in **boldface**.

- Underlined letters in menu names, menu commands, and dialog box options appear in **boldface**. Examples are **F**ile menu, **O**pen command, and **C**ommand Line text box.

- Important words or phrases are in *italic* the first time they are discussed.

- Screen displays and messages appear in a `special font`.

- *Key terms* in the margins are briefly defined as they are introduced.

- *Notes* provide information that might help you avoid problems or accomplish tasks more efficiently.

- *Cautions* in the margins contain information about potential problems or errors.

- *If you have problems...* paragraphs provide troubleshooting information to help you avoid or escape problem situations.

In this book, you *choose* or *click* commands and buttons in dialog boxes, and you *select* or *click* items in lists on-screen.

As with all Windows applications, you can use the mouse, the keyboard, or shortcut keys for most operations in the Windows program. In some cases, you may need to use key combinations. In this book, a key combination is joined by a plus sign (+). For example, Alt+Tab means that you are to hold down the Alt key, press the Tab key, and then release both keys.

Both Windows and DOS accept commands and file names in uppercase or lowercase sequences or combinations, but many Windows applications have functions that are case sensitive. You should type proper names, addresses, and so on, with the correct case in Write, Cardfile, Calendar, and other Windows programs. You can generally use any case combination you like in dialog boxes or commands.

Part I
Getting Started with Windows

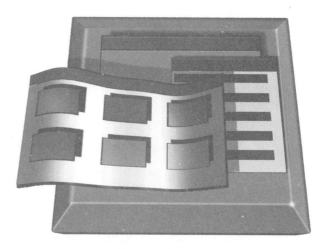

Lesson 1

Learning the Basics

This lesson introduces you to Windows. You will start the Windows program, learn how to use a mouse, explore the menu system, and learn about the different parts of a dialog box. This lesson also covers use of the Windows on-line Help facility. The final section discusses how to exit the Windows program properly before turning off your computer.

Before you start this lesson, you should have Windows installed on your system. If you need assistance with the installation process, turn to Appendix A, "Installing Windows 3.11 or Windows for Workgroups 3.11."

In this lesson, you learn to

- Start the Windows program

- Identify parts of the Program Manager window

- Use the mouse within Windows

- Open the pull-down menus and choose menu commands

- Make selections in dialog boxes

- Access the Help system

- Exit the Windows program

Disk operating system (DOS)
Acts as an interpreter between you and your computer, translating your commands into computer language.

Introducing Windows 3.11

Windows is an environment surrounding the *disk operating system* (DOS). DOS enables programs to run on your computer. Before Windows, computer users had to remember difficult DOS commands. Users also needed to learn DOS-based programs such as Lotus 1-2-3 and WordPerfect, which had no common menu structure or operating techniques. Much practice was necessary to become proficient in DOS-based programs, and hard work was required to master the power hidden inside them. Windows eliminates these problems. Windows masks DOS, doing away with arcane DOS commands and improving the way programs use memory.

Graphical user interface (GUI)
A visual environment that helps you manage your computer programs more easily and with more consistency.

People are visual creatures; most of what we learn comes through our sight. Both Windows and Windows programs use what is technically known as a *graphical user interface*, or GUI (pronounced "gooey"). A GUI takes advantage of the visual way in which people are accustomed to working (and prefer to work).

Programs designed specifically for Windows—such as Microsoft Excel, Aldus PageMaker, and WordPerfect for Windows—use menus and dialog boxes that operate in much the same way. Learning one program, therefore, helps you learn other Windows programs. And because menus and dialog boxes make all options available to beginners as well as experts, Windows programs are more accessible to all users. Everyone moves up the productivity curve.

Task: Start Windows

Some computers are set up to start Windows automatically when you turn them on. Your system may have a menu from which you can choose the Windows program. If this is the case, you can skip these instructions and proceed to the next section, "Understanding the Program Manager Window."

To start Windows, follow these steps:

1. Turn on your computer and monitor.

2. Wait until the DOS prompt appears. It probably looks something like this: c:>.

3. Type **win**.

4. Press Enter.

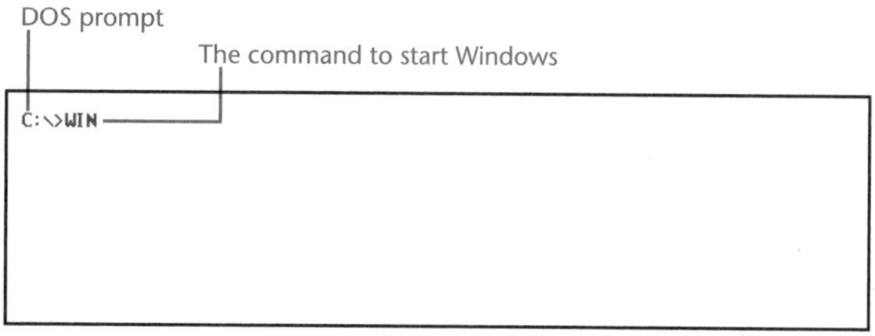

DOS prompt

The command to start Windows

```
C:\>WIN
```

You start Windows just as you start any other DOS program, by typing the appropriate command at the DOS prompt.

If you have problems...

If Windows does not start, a couple of things could be wrong. First, the Windows program might not be installed on your system. Second, the location of the Windows directory might not be specified in the AUTOEXEC.BAT file (a system file).

Check whether Windows is installed. Type **cd\windows** at the DOS prompt. If the prompt changes to C:\WINDOWS>, the problem is in the AUTOEXEC.BAT file. Type **win** to start the program.

If you get the message Invalid directory, the Windows program has not been installed. See Appendix A, "Installing Windows 3.11 or Windows for Workgroups 3.11," for assistance with installation.

Desktop
The background in Windows on which your windows and icons appear.

Window
An on-screen box that can contain application and group icons, open applications, or documents.

Icon
A small graphic image representing an application, document, or other object.

Understanding the Program Manager Window

When you start the Windows program, a banner displays for a few seconds, and then Program Manager appears. As the name implies, Program Manager manages the programs on your computer (both DOS and Windows programs).

In Windows, the computer screen is called a *desktop*. The accompanying figure shows Program Manager in a *window* on the desktop. Program Manager contains application *icons*, which represent your *applications*, and group icons, which represent groups of applications. When you select a group icon, it opens into a window that displays the application icons within that group.

You start all applications from the Program Manager window.

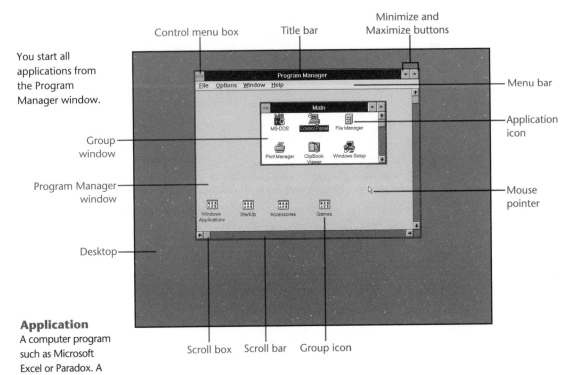

Control menu box · Title bar · Minimize and Maximize buttons

Menu bar

Group window

Application icon

Program Manager window

Mouse pointer

Desktop

Scroll box · Scroll bar · Group icon

Application
A computer program such as Microsoft Excel or Paradox. A program is a set of instructions that tells the computer what to do.

Note: *You can create your own group icons and application icons. In addition, you can customize your desktop to automatically display the group windows you use most often (see Lesson 3, "Working with Groups and Applications").*

If you have problems...

Don't be concerned if your screen doesn't match the one shown in the figure. You successfully started the program, and that's the most important thing. Lessons 3 and 5 should answer any questions you have about customizing your desktop.

If you don't see Program Manager at all, look in the bottom-left corner of the screen for a small Program Manager icon. Press Enter to display the Program Manager window.

The Title Bar

All Windows programs display a title bar across the top of each window. The title bar shows the name of the window, application, or document. Because Program Manager is displayed in the window, the words Program Manager appear in the title bar.

The title bar also contains a Control menu box and Minimize and Maximize buttons. These are discussed in Lesson 2, "Working with Windows."

The Menu Bar

The menu bar appears directly below the title bar. The menu bar lists four menus: **F**ile, **O**ptions, **W**indow, and **H**elp. Three of these menus—**F**ile, **W**indow, and **H**elp—appear in every Windows program. You can access the menu bar with either the mouse or the keyboard.

Application Icons

Every application in Windows has an icon assigned to it. Application icons are placed in group windows, which are represented by group icons. To start an application, simply choose the application's icon.

Note: *You can copy application icons into the StartUp group window. Thereafter, those applications start automatically when you start Windows. See Lesson 4, "Starting and Controlling Applications," for more information.*

Group Icons

In Windows, applications are organized into groups. Each group has a program group window that opens when you choose the group icon. You can easily move and copy application icons between program group windows. The Applications, Main, Games, Accessories, and StartUp groups are created when you install Windows. Table 1.1 describes the functions of these groups.

Table 1.1 Group Windows Created during Installation of Windows	
Group Window	**Description**
Main	Includes programs and tools to help you control printing; set up printers, plotters, and modems; customize the desktop; and manage files.
Accessories	Includes desktop programs that come with Windows, such as a simple word processing program, a drawing program, a calendar, and a calculator.
StartUp	A group window in which you can add programs that start automatically when you start Windows. This window is empty until you add programs.

(continues)

Table 1.1 Continued	
Group Window	**Description**
Games	Includes two games—Solitaire and Minesweeper—that you can use to practice your mouse skills.
Applications	Includes any applications that Windows detects on your hard disk during installation.

Task: Use the Mouse

Windows is designed to be used with a mouse, but you can also use the function keys and shortcut keys. This book concentrates on mouse techniques; if a keyboard technique is faster, it will be mentioned in a note.

Your mouse may have two or three buttons. Some Windows applications use the right button (and the middle button on a three-button mouse) although this use is rare. The left button is called the *primary mouse button* because you use it most of the time. Unless you are instructed otherwise, use the left button throughout the lessons in this book.

A mouse has many functions in Windows and Windows programs. You can use the mouse to choose items such as application or program icons, choose options in dialog boxes, and execute menu commands. You can use the mouse also to move and resize objects quickly.

Note: *If you are left-handed, you can switch the mouse buttons. This procedure is discussed in Lesson 5, "Personalizing Windows."*

To use the mouse, follow these steps:

1. Place your hand on the mouse, with two fingers resting on the buttons.

2. Slowly slide the mouse across your desk (or mouse pad, if you have one). As you slide the mouse, the mouse pointer moves on-screen.

The mouse pointer looks like an arrowhead (see the preceding figure) but may change shape, depending on the task. Later lessons in this book explain these different shapes.

1

Note: *Most mouse users prefer sliding the mouse across a mouse pad to using the slick surfaces of their desks. A mouse pad provides more friction, which makes the mouse movement smoother. You can purchase mouse pads at an office supply or computer store.*

Table 1.2 describes the four basic mouse operations used in Windows programs.

Table 1.2 Basic Mouse Operations	
Operation	**Description**
Point	Move the mouse pointer so that it touches an item on-screen.
Click	Lightly press and release a mouse button (unless otherwise indicated, the left mouse button).
Double-click	Press and release the left mouse button twice in rapid succession.
Drag	Press and hold down the left mouse button while moving the mouse to a different location.

Other pointing devices are available. The most popular is the trackball, commonly found on laptop computers. A stylus pen can also be used on a monitor's screen or on a graphics tablet to select menu options.

Using Menus and Dialog Boxes

One of the major advantages of using Windows is the consistent interface it offers. All Windows programs follow the same standard of operation; all the menus, commands, and dialog boxes work the same way. While you learn how to use one Windows program, you are learning skills that will help you operate other Windows programs.

Pull-down menu
A menu that cascades down into the screen from the menu bar when you open, or "pull down," the menu.

Menus

Windows commands are organized in *pull-down menus*. You pull down, or open, a menu by clicking a menu name in the menu bar, located directly below the title bar. The menu name usually describes the type of commands within that menu. After you open a menu, you can choose a command from the list.

When a list of menu commands is displayed, you will notice that symbols appear beside some commands. The accompanying figure illustrates and explains these symbols.

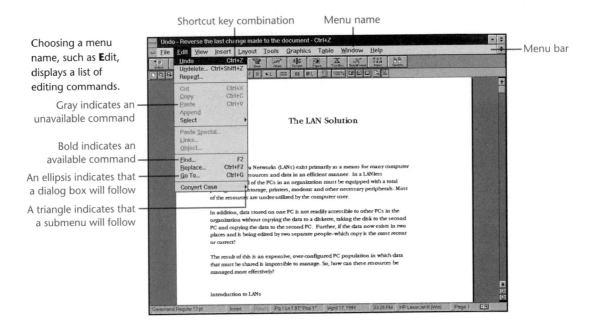

Shortcut key combination

Menu name

Choosing a menu name, such as **E**dit, displays a list of editing commands.

Menu bar

Gray indicates an unavailable command

Bold indicates an available command

An ellipsis indicates that a dialog box will follow

A triangle indicates that a submenu will follow

You can use either the mouse or the keyboard to make selections from menus. As noted, this book emphasizes use of the mouse.

Follow these steps to open a menu and choose a command from the menu:

1. Place the mouse pointer on the menu name.

2. Click the mouse button.

3. Place the mouse pointer on the menu command.

4. Click the mouse button.

Note: *You can press Alt plus the underlined letter in any menu name to open that menu. Alternatively, you can use the down-arrow key to highlight the menu command, and then press Enter.*

Dialog Boxes

Dialog box
A box that appears when Windows wants to communicate a message or when you need to specify more information to execute a command.

Many menu commands require additional information before they can perform an operation. These command names are followed by an ellipsis (...) in the menus. A *dialog box* appears after you choose one of these commands, enabling you to specify the necessary information. An example is the Run dialog box, in which you specify the file name for the program you want to execute. The next figures illustrate various options available in dialog boxes.

In this dialog box, the Run **M**inimized check box is empty, indicating that the option is not selected.

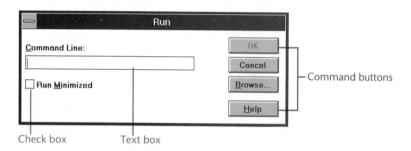

Check box   Text box   Command buttons

In this dialog box, the Program **G**roup option button is filled, indicating that the option is selected.

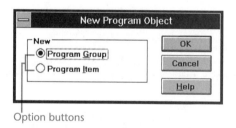

Option buttons

This dialog box shows a text box where you can type information, as well as a list box and drop-down list where you can select from a list of predefined options.

Text box

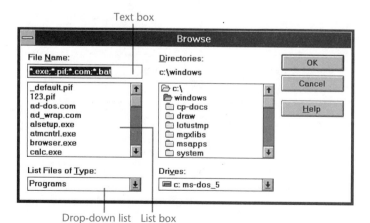

Drop-down list   List box

Most dialog boxes use list boxes and drop-down lists whenever possible to make selecting easier. A drop-down list conserves space by not showing the full list until you select it. Table 1.3 provides brief descriptions of elements found in dialog boxes.

Table 1.3 Dialog Box Elements	
Element	**Description**
Command button	A button that you click to execute a command or to display another dialog box.
Text box	An area where you can type information, such as a file name.
Check box	A square box that displays an X if the option is turned on. You can select more than one check box.
Option button	A round button that specifies one option in a group of options. You can select only one button in the group, and the selected button is filled. (Option buttons are sometimes called radio buttons.)
List box	A list of predefined options. (List boxes are also used for lists of files and directories.)
Drop-down list	A list of predefined options that you open by clicking the underlined arrow next to the list.

Using the mouse is the easiest way to make selections in a dialog box. The following steps describe how to select each dialog box element.

To select a command button:

1. Place the mouse pointer on the button.

2. Click the mouse button.

Note: *To select a command button with the keyboard, use the Tab key to move through the buttons. When the command button that you want has a bold outline, press Enter.*

If you have problems... If you click the mouse button and nothing happens, make sure that the pointer is directly on top of the button on-screen, not on a border of the button. Place the mouse pointer in the middle of the button and try again.

To activate a text box:

1. Place the mouse pointer inside the text box. The mouse pointer should change to an I-beam.

2. Click the mouse button.

3. Type the new text or edit the existing entry.

Note: *To activate a text box with the keyboard, hold down the Alt key and press the underlined letter in the text box's label.*

If you have problems...	If you have trouble selecting the text box, wait until the mouse pointer changes to an I-beam before clicking the mouse button.

To select a check box:

1. Place the mouse pointer on the check box or the item name.

2. Click the mouse button. An X should appear in the check box.

Note: *To select a check box with the keyboard, hold down the Alt key and press the underlined letter in the item name.*

If you have problems...	If an X doesn't appear in the check box, you have not selected it. Make sure that you are placing the mouse pointer directly on top of the check box or item name before clicking the mouse button.

To deselect a check box:

1. Place the mouse pointer on the check box or the item name.

2. Click the mouse button. The X should no longer appear in the check box.

To select an option button:

1. Place the mouse pointer on the option button or the item name.

2. Click the mouse button.

Note: To select an option button with the keyboard, hold down the Alt key and press the underlined letter in the item name.

If you have problems...

If the option button doesn't turn black, you have not selected it. Make sure that you are placing the mouse pointer directly on top of the option button or the item name before clicking the mouse button.

To make a selection from a list box:

Scroll bar
A bar that appears at the bottom or right side of a window when the window is not large enough to display all the contents.

1. If necessary, scroll through the list by clicking the up or down arrow on the *scroll bar* located on the right side of the list box.

2. Click the item in the list. The selected item appears highlighted.

Note: To activate a list box with the keyboard, press Alt plus the underlined letter in the list box's label. Then use the up- and down-arrow keys to scroll through the list until the item that you want is highlighted. Finally, press Enter to select the item.

If you have problems...

If you can't see the item you want in the list, make sure that you have scrolled completely through all the items. If the list is long, click the top or bottom scroll arrow and hold down the mouse button to scroll quickly through the list. See "Task: Using Scroll Bars" in Lesson 2.

To make a selection from a drop-down list:

1. Open the list by clicking the underlined arrow beside the list.

2. If necessary, scroll through the list by clicking the up or down arrow in the scroll bar on the right side of the list box.

3. Click the item you want in the list. The selected item appears highlighted.

4. To cancel the drop-down list without making a change, click the underlined down arrow beside the list again.

1

Note: *To activate a drop-down list with the keyboard, press Alt plus the underlined letter in the drop-down list's label. Press Alt+down arrow to move into the list; then use the up- or down-arrow key to highlight an item. Press Enter to select the highlighted item.*

If you have problems...

If you can't see the item you want in the list, check that you have scrolled completely through all the items. If the list is long, click the top or bottom scroll arrow and hold down the mouse button to scroll quickly through the list.

To cancel a dialog box without making any changes, click the Cancel command button or press Esc. You can also double-click the Control menu box for the dialog box.

Task: Make Selections in Menus and Dialog Boxes

Remember that all Windows programs use the same type of menus and dialog boxes. Because all levels of commands are easily available, even a beginner can perform complex tasks quickly.

Follow these steps to make selections in menus and dialog boxes:

1. Click **F**ile in the menu bar to pull down the **F**ile menu. Read through the **F**ile menu commands.

The commands in the **F**ile menu manage program groups and program items in Program Manager.

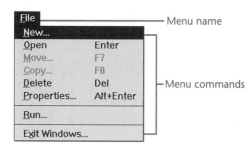

2. Click **O**ptions to open the **O**ptions menu. Read through the **O**ptions menu commands. Notice the check mark next to the **S**ave Settings on Exit option. The check mark means that the option is selected.

The **S**ave Settings on Exit option saves the current Program Manager settings for the next time you start Windows.

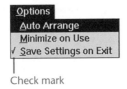

Check mark

3. Click **S**ave Settings on Exit to *deselect* (turn off) the option.

4. Click **F**ile in the menu bar to open the **F**ile menu.

5. Click **N**ew to open the New Program Object dialog box.

6. Click the Program **G**roup option button. This option creates a new program group.

The filled option button indicates which option is selected.

Selected option button

Unselected option button

Click here to cancel this dialog box

7. Click the Program **I**tem option button. Notice that only one of the two option buttons can be selected.

8. Click the Cancel command button to cancel the New Program Object dialog box.

Using the Windows Help System

The Windows program comes with an extensive Help facility to assist you when you have questions about the application. The Help system is on-line and *context sensitive*, which means that you can display specific help for the task you are trying to do. Windows Help includes a tutorial that introduces you to Windows.

To access the Help system, follow these steps:

1. Place the mouse pointer on **H**elp in the menu bar.

2. Click the left mouse button.

Note: If you press F1, the Contents screen for the Help system appears. If you press F1 while a menu is displayed, a help screen for that menu appears.

The Help menu includes **C**ontents and **S**earch commands that help you access the correct help screen quickly.

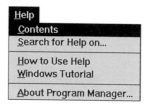

Table 1.4 describes the menu commands available in the Program Manager **H**elp menu.

Table 1.4 Help Menu Options	
Option	**Description**
Contents	Displays a list of available help subjects. Choose one of the listed subjects to jump to that subject.
Search for Help On	Displays an alphabetic list of key words and phrases found in the help topics. You can type a word and search through the list, or select a topic from the list to move to that topic.
How to Use Help	Displays a list of topics on using the Help system.
Windows Tutorial	Runs a short tutorial program that introduces you to Windows.
About Program Manager	Indicates your Windows version number and to whom this copy of Windows is licensed. Also displays the amount of memory and system resources available. This is necessary information when you call Microsoft for technical support.

When you select a help topic, the Program Manager Help window opens, displaying a help screen for that topic. The Help window has its own title bar and menu bar. Below the menu bar is a button bar that contains a series of command buttons.

Command button   Help menu bar   Help button bar   Help title bar

Command buttons
make it easy to
navigate through
the Help system.
Simply click the
appropriate button
to select it.

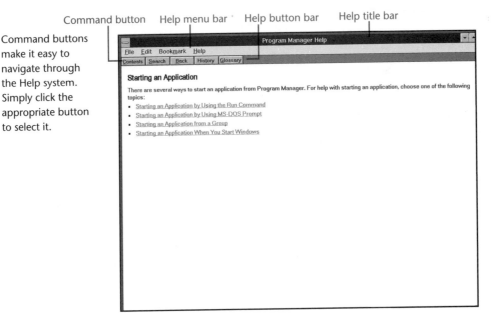

Table 1.5 describes the command buttons in the Program Manager Help window.

Table 1.5 Help Command Buttons	
Button	**Description**
Contents	Displays a list of available help subjects. Choose one of the listed subjects to jump to that subject.
Search	Displays an alphabetic list of key words and phrases found in the help topics. You can type a word and search through the list, or you can select a topic from the list to move to that topic.
Back	Moves backward through the help topics you have viewed, until you reach the Contents screen.
His**t**ory	Displays a list of the last 40 help topics you have viewed, with the most recent topic at the top of the list. You can return to a topic quickly by selecting it from the list.
Glossary	Displays an alphabetic list of terms used in the Help system. Select a term to display the definition.

Task: View Help Contents

To get an overview of your program or to see what subjects are contained in the Help system, you can list the Help system contents.

To view the contents, follow these steps:

1. Pull down the **H**elp menu by clicking **H**elp in the menu bar.

   Note: *If you are already in the Help system, you can click the **C**ontents button in the button bar.*

2. Choose **C**ontents (click the menu command).

In the Help system list of contents, subjects are divided into two categories: How To and Commands.

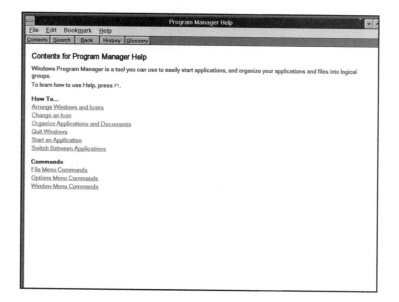

The subjects in the How To category describe how to perform functions in Program Manager. The subjects in the Commands category describe how the commands in Program Manager's three menus work. Note that the subjects are shown in green.

To jump to a Help subject, just click the subject. Note that in the Help contents list the mouse pointer changes to a hand with a pointing finger.

Note: *Alternatively, you can press the Tab key until the subject is highlighted and then press Enter.*

Task: Search for Help on Specific Topics

In the Help system, you can click the **S**earch button when you want to search for help on a specific topic. In Program Manager, for example, you can follow these steps to search for topics related to starting applications:

1. Click the **S**earch button to display the Search dialog box.

2. In the text box, type **applications, starting**.

   or

   Click the down arrow in the scroll bar until `applications, starting` appears in the list; then click that phrase.

   Note: *You can also press Tab to move into the list, and then press the down-arrow key to select* `applications, starting`. *Press Enter to list the available topics.*

In the Search dialog box, `applications, starting` is selected as the search topic.

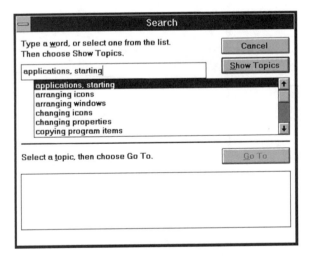

3. Click the **S**how Topics button in the upper-right corner of the dialog box.

4. In the Select a **T**opic text box, click the topic for which you want information.

5. Click the **G**o To button to go to the topic.

All topics that are related to the word or phrase you typed appear in the topic list at the bottom of the dialog box.

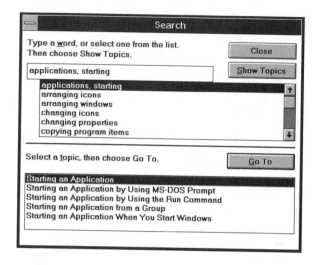

Note: *In some Windows programs, pressing Shift+F1 changes the mouse pointer to a question mark. If you then click a command or a particular part of the screen, Help displays information about that command or that portion of the screen.*

Task: Jump to Another Help Topic

Hypertext

A nonsequential method for retrieving information. The reader can jump to topics not necessarily in a particular order.

Within the Help text are underlined *hypertext* words or phrases that enable you to jump to related information. Two kinds of underlines are used for hypertext words and phrases in Help text:

Underline	Action You Take
Solid underline	Click the word or phrase with a solid underline to jump to that topic. Click the **B**ack button to return to the preceding topic.
Dashed underline	Click the word or phrase with a dashed underline to display the definition (click a second time to close the definition).

Task: Exit the Help System

When you are finished using Help, you can either exit the Help system or leave it open in case you need to use it again. If you want to leave the Help system open, just click anywhere in the application window. This hides the Help window *behind* the application window so that it's out of your way. Otherwise, follow these steps to close the Help system:

1. Pull down the **F**ile menu by clicking **F**ile in the menu bar.

2. Choose E**x**it (click the menu command).

Task: Exit Windows

Program Manager controls Windows, so when you close the Program Manager window, you exit Windows.

Follow these steps to exit Windows:

1. Click **F**ile in the menu bar to pull down the **F**ile menu.

2. Choose E**x**it Windows (click the menu command).

    A dialog box appears in the middle of the screen, asking you to confirm the E**x**it command.

3. Click OK.

Note: *To exit Windows, you can also double-click the Control menu box for Program Manager.*

Note: *There are two keyboard techniques for exiting Windows. First, you can activate the Program Control menu in the Program Manager window (press Alt+space bar) and choose the **C**lose command. Second, you can press Alt+F4 to close Windows. Note that these techniques can be used to close any window.*

Summary

To	Do This
Start Windows	Type **win** at the DOS prompt.
Move the mouse pointer	Slide the mouse across your desk or mouse pad.
Click	Press and release the left mouse button.

To	Do This
Double-click	Press and release the left mouse button twice in rapid succession.
Drag	Press and hold down the left mouse button while moving the mouse to a different location.
Open a menu	Click the menu name in the menu bar.
Choose a menu command	Click the menu command.
Select a command button in a dialog box	Click the command button.
Select a text box in a dialog box	Click the text box.
Select (or deselect) a check box in a dialog box	Click the check box or the item name.
Select an option button	Click the option button or the item name.
Make a selection from a list box	Click the item in the list. If necessary, click the up or down arrow in the scroll bar to move through the list.
Make a selection from a drop-down list	Click the underlined arrow beside the list and then click the item in the list. If necessary, click the up or down arrow in the scroll bar to scroll through the list.
Cancel a dialog box	Click the Cancel command button or press Esc.
Get help	Pull down the **H**elp menu by clicking **H**elp in the menu bar.
Display the Help Contents screen	From outside the Help system, pull down the **H**elp menu and choose **C**ontents. Or press F1. From within the Help system, click the **C**ontents button.
Search for a Help topic	From outside the Help system, pull down the **H**elp menu and choose **S**earch for Help On. From within the Help system, click the **S**earch button.
Run the Windows tutorial	Pull down the **H**elp menu and choose **W**indows Tutorial.
Display the Windows version and license information	Pull down the **H**elp menu and choose **A**bout Program Manager.

On Your Own
Estimated time: 15 minutes

To get started with Windows, follow these steps:

1. Start Windows.

2. Pull down each of the menus in the menu bar and take note of the commands in each menu.

3. Open the Browse dialog box by choosing **F**ile, **R**un, and **B**rowse.

4. Practice moving through the list boxes and drop-down lists.

5. Cancel the Browse dialog box without making any changes.

6. Use the Help system to learn more about Program Manager.

7. Search for help on group icons.

8. Use the **B**ack command button to move backward through the help topics you have viewed.

9. Exit the Help system.

10. Use context-sensitive help to display a help screen for the New Program Object dialog box. *(Hint:* To open the dialog box, pull down the **F**ile menu and choose **N**ew.)

11. Display your Windows version and license information. Take note of the available memory and system resources information at the bottom of the dialog box.

12. Exit Windows.

Working with Windows

Most of us organize projects on our desks by allocating space and arranging the projects according to their importance. The same technique can be used to set up windows on the Windows desktop. Program Manager is in a window, and your programs are organized into windows. All these windows can be moved around and sized so that you can quickly locate the programs you use most.

In this lesson, you learn how to move and size windows on the Windows desktop to accommodate your unique work habits. Specifically, you learn to

- ■ Identify the Minimize, Maximize, and Restore buttons
- ■ Locate the Control menu commands
- ■ Minimize, maximize, and restore windows
- ■ Move and resize windows
- ■ Use scroll bars
- ■ View multiple group windows

Minimizing, Maximizing, and Restoring Windows

Minimize

To shrink a window so that it is represented as an icon.

Most windows (group, program, and document) have *Minimize* and *Maximize* buttons located on the right side of the title bar. A *Restore* button appears in place of the Maximize button when a window has been maximized. In addition, a Control menu containing the Minimize, Maximize, and **R**estore commands is available when you click the Control menu box, located on the left side of the title bar.

You can use the choices on the Control menu or use the Minimize, Maximize, and Restore buttons to control windows.

Control menu box

Control menu

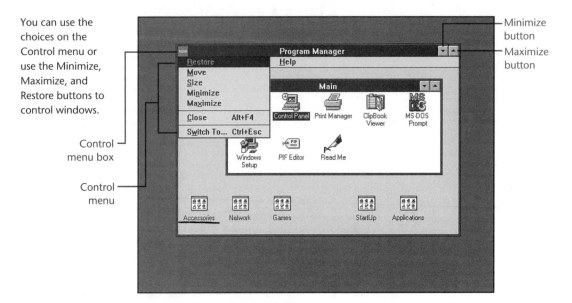

Minimize button

Maximize button

Maximize
To expand a program or document window so that it fills the screen.

Restore
To restore a program or document window to its original size before it was maximized or minimized.

The techniques discussed in this lesson can also be used on document windows in other Windows applications. Depending on the application, a document window might contain a word processing document, a spreadsheet, or a drawing. As you will see in later lessons, document windows have their own Minimize, Maximize, and Restore buttons as well as Control menu boxes. If the document window is maximized, these options are located on the far left and right sides of the *menu* bar. If the window is not maximized, these options are located on the document window's title bar.

Task: Maximize Program Manager

Program Manager itself is in a window, so you control Program Manager as you would any other window. When Program Manager is maximized, you have the maximum amount of workspace for the group windows.

To maximize Program Manager (to make it full-screen size), click the Maximize button (up arrow) on the right side of the Program Manager title bar. Or click the Control menu box on the left side of the Program Manager title bar and then click the Ma**x**imize command.

Note: *Alternatively, you can press Alt+space bar to open the Control menu.*

Program Manager completely covers the desktop so that the maximum amount of application workspace is available.

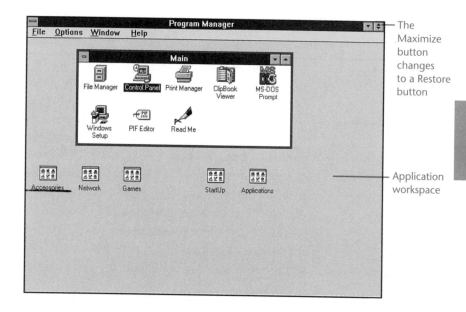

The Maximize button changes to a Restore button

Application workspace

If you have problems...

If you accidentally click the Minimize button, you will reduce Program Manager to an icon. To restore Program Manager to a window, double-click the icon.

If you accidentally click the Maximize button for a group window, you will maximize the group window on top of Program Manager. To restore the group window, click the Restore button on the far right side of the *menu* bar.

Task: Restore Maximized Program Manager

When you maximize a window, the Maximize button changes to a Restore button, which displays both an up arrow and a down arrow. The Restore button will shrink the window to its original size before you maximized it. For example, if you are looking for an infrequently used program in a group window, you may want to maximize the group window so that you can see all the application icons. When you are finished looking, use the Restore button to restore the window to its original size.

To restore the Program Manager window, click the Restore button (up and down arrows) on the right side of the Program Manager title bar. Or click the Control menu box on the left side of the Program Manager title bar and then click the **R**estore command.

> **Note:** *Alternatively, you can press Alt+space bar to open the Control menu.*

**If you have
problems...**

If you accidentally click the Minimize button, you will reduce Program Manager to an icon. To restore Program Manager to a window, double-click the icon.

Task: Minimize Program Manager

When you are working with several programs at once, you may want to reduce some of them to icons. An icon requires less space on-screen and can easily be restored to a window or maximized to full-screen. Notice that some of the group window icons in your Program Manager window are minimized to icons. It is useful to leave rarely used group windows as icons so that you have more room to open group windows you use frequently.

To minimize the Program Manager window, click the Minimize button (down arrow) on the right side of the Program Manager title bar. Or click the Control menu box on the left side of the Program Manager title bar and then click the Minimize command.

Note: *Alternatively, you can press Alt+space bar to open the Control menu.*

Program Manager is
shown as an icon
on the desktop.

Program Manager icon

If you have problems...

If you accidentally click the Maximize button, you will expand the Program Manager window to full-screen. Try again to click the Minimize button.

If you click the Minimize button for a group window, you will reduce that group window to an icon. Make sure that you click the Minimize button on the Program Manager title bar.

Task: Restore Minimized Program Manager

When you minimize a window to an icon, you no longer have access to the Control menu box or the Minimize and Maximize buttons. Note that while you do not have access to the Control menu *box*, you can still access the Control menu.

To restore the Program Manager icon to a window, double-click the Program Manager icon. You can also click the Program Manager icon (which opens the Control menu) and then click the **R**estore command.

If you have problems...

If you double-click the icon and nothing happens, you may not be double-clicking fast enough. Try the double-click again. If it still doesn't work, click the icon once and then click the **R**estore command on the Control menu.

Task: Minimize, Maximize, and Restore Group Windows

Group window
A window represented by a group icon and containing related application icons.

Group windows have their own set of Minimize and Maximize buttons as well as a Control menu box on the title bar. A group window can be maximized on top of Program Manager. When this happens, the name of the group window is added to the Program Manager title bar, and the Restore button and Control menu box are placed on the menu bar. This arrangement is similar to the way document windows inside an application window operate. The Restore button and the Control menu box on the menu bar control the window listed *second* in the title bar. These same options on the title bar represent the window listed *first* in the title bar.

Note that the Control menu box for Program Manager is different from the Control menu box for the group window. The horizontal bar for the Program Manager Control menu is larger and is intended to resemble a space bar. As noted, the keyboard shortcut for opening the Control menu is Alt+space bar. The horizontal bar for the group window Control menu is smaller and is intended to resemble the hyphen or minus key. Therefore, the keyboard shortcut for opening this Control menu is Alt+hyphen.

Follow these steps to maximize, restore, and minimize a group window:

1. Double-click the Accessories group icon (or any other group icon) to open the group window.

   or

   Pull down the **W**indow menu (click **W**indow on the menu bar) and click the group name (Accessories) in the list of group windows.

   The group window opens and shows you the application icons contained within it. A scroll bar may be displayed if there are more icons than can fit in the group window.

2. Click the Maximize button to maximize the group window on top of Program Manager.

   Notice the change in the title bar, as well as the Control menu box and Restore button on the menu bar.

The Accessories group window has icons for all the supplementary programs included with the Windows program.

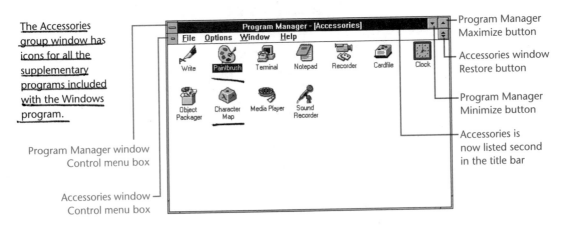

Program Manager window Control menu box

Accessories window Control menu box

Program Manager Maximize button

Accessories window Restore button

Program Manager Minimize button

Accessories is now listed second in the title bar

3. Click the Restore button on the far right side of the menu bar to restore the Accessories window.

4. Click the Minimize button on the Accessories title bar to minimize the window to an icon.

Note: *A rule of thumb is that the Control menu box and the Minimize, Maximize, and Restore buttons on the title bar control Program Manager or the open application. The same features on the menu bar control only the group or document window.*

If you have problems...

Make sure that you are using the correct Control menu box and Minimize, Maximize, and Restore buttons. The options on the title bar control the Program Manager window. The options on the menu bar control the group window currently open on top of Program Manager.

Resizing and Moving Windows

Restore mode

The mode in which a window is neither maximized nor minimized.

As you have already seen, you can maximize a window to full-screen or shrink it to an icon. When not minimized or maximized, the window is in *restore mode*. Restored windows can be sized to show only those programs that you use often. Restored windows can also be moved around on the desktop, just as you position paper documents on your desk according to how often you use them.

Task: Resize a Window

A window in restore mode has a border around it. You can click and drag the window border and stretch it to increase or decrease the size of the window. When you point to the window border, the mouse pointer changes to a double-headed arrow. When you see the double-headed arrow, you can click and drag the border to stretch it. A dotted guide line will appear to show how the window will look when you release the mouse button.

Note: *Not every window can be resized—only those with a sizeable border. A sizeable border has a thick border composed of two thin black lines with a color fill. A nonsizeable border is a single thin black line.*

The double-headed arrow indicates the direction in which you can size the window. For example, pointing to the bottom of the border will change the pointer to a double-headed arrow that points up and down. You can click and drag the top, bottom, left, and right borders. You can also click and drag a border corner to alter the size in two directions at once.

Follow these steps to resize the Program Manager window:

1. If Program Manager is maximized, click the Restore button in the upper-right corner of the title bar.

2. If Program Manager is minimized to an icon, double-click the icon.

3. Point to the bottom of the border until the mouse pointer changes to a double-headed arrow.

4. Click and hold down the mouse button.

5. Move the mouse down to lengthen the window.

Moving the mouse
down lengthens the
window; moving
the mouse up
shortens the
window.

Old window border ———

Guide line ———

Double-headed arrow ———

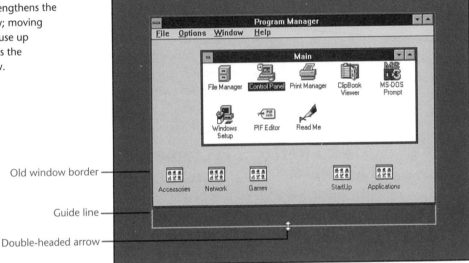

6. Release the mouse button.

7. Point to the bottom-left corner of the border until the pointer changes to a diagonal double-headed arrow.

8. Click and drag the corner. Notice how the size changes depending on where you move the mouse.

9. When you are satisfied with the size of the Program Manager window, release the mouse button.

If you have problems...

If you can't get the mouse pointer to change to a double-headed arrow, you probably need to slow down a bit. If you slide the mouse pointer across the border too quickly, the pointer will change to the double-headed arrow and then back to the normal arrow. Place the tip of the mouse pointer on the border and drag down *very slowly*.

If you can't get the dotted guide line to appear, you may be releasing the mouse button too soon. When the mouse pointer changes, click and hold down the button firmly. Now slowly move the mouse—you should see the dotted guide line. Don't release the mouse button until you are finished resizing.

Task: Use Scroll Bars

Scroll bar
A bar that appears at the bottom or right side of a window when the contents of the window are not completely visible.

Resizing windows may cause some of your icons to disappear. Notice that if the window is too small to display all the icons it contains, *scroll bars* will appear. A horizontal scroll bar appears at the bottom of the window if the additional icons can be found to the left or right. A vertical scroll bar appears at the right side of the window if the additional icons are above or below the currently displayed icons.

A scroll bar includes a *scroll box* and *scroll arrows*. Scroll bars are used to move through a window to locate additional items that do not appear initially.

Scroll box
A small box in the scroll bar. Drag the scroll box to move quickly through a window.

Note: *The position of the scroll box on the scroll bar indicates your relative position in the window.*

Follow these steps to scroll through a window:

1. Using the techniques described in the preceding section, reduce the size of the Main window so that both the horizontal and vertical scroll bars appear.

Scroll bars appear automatically if you size a window in such a way that all the contents are not visible.

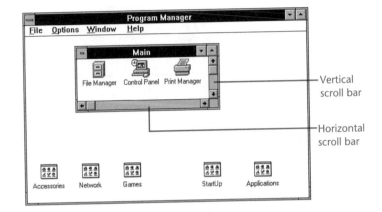

Vertical scroll bar

Horizontal scroll bar

Scroll arrow
An arrow at either end of a scroll bar. Click the arrow or click and hold down the arrow to move through the window.

2. Click the down arrow on the vertical scroll bar to move down through the window until you reach the bottom. Note that the scroll box has moved down to the bottom of the scroll bar, indicating that you are at the bottom of the window.

3. Click the up arrow on the vertical scroll bar to move back to the top of the window.

4. Click the right arrow on the horizontal scroll bar to move to the right corner of the window.

5. Click and drag the scroll box on the horizontal scroll bar to move back to the left corner of the window.

6. Click the area on the vertical scroll bar between the scroll box and the down arrow to move down through the window.

7. Finally, resize the Main group window so that all the icons are visible again.

Task: Move a Window

You can move the Program Manager window around on the desktop, and you can move the group windows around in the Program Manager window. As with resizing a window, the window must be in restore mode before you can move it.

Follow these steps to move a window:

1. If no group windows are displayed, double-click the Main group icon to open the Main group window (or use an existing open group window).

2. Place the mouse pointer in the Main group window title bar.

3. Click and hold down the mouse button; then slowly move the mouse down.

A dotted guide line appears so that you can see where the window will be when you release the mouse button.

Click and drag the title bar to move the window

Dotted guide line

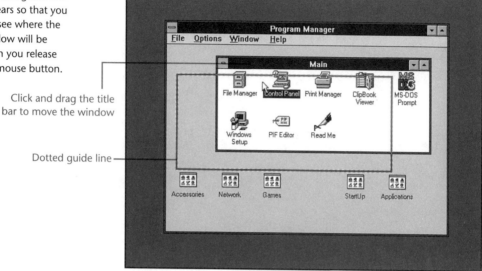

4. Release the mouse button when you are satisfied with the position.

5. Double-click the Games group icon to open the Games window.

6. Click and drag the title bar to move the Games window.

7. Click the Minimize button to minimize the Games window.

8. Double-click the Games group icon to open the Games window again.

Notice how the window is restored to the exact position where you moved it in the previous step.

All dialog boxes are displayed in windows that can be moved on-screen. For example, if you are spell-checking a document and the Speller dialog box is blocking your view of the text, you can click and drag the title bar of the dialog box to move it out of the way.

Viewing Multiple Windows

Application workspace
The open space in the middle of the Program Manager window where group windows can be arranged.

You can open multiple group windows at the same time. The only limit is the amount of *application workspace* in the Program Manager window. Maximizing the Program Manager window gives the maximum amount of space for your group windows.

Task: Arrange Multiple Windows Manually

Group windows containing frequently used programs should be sized and positioned on-screen so that you can quickly locate those program icons. Both document and application windows can be resized and moved so that you can view multiple windows simultaneously. Viewing multiple windows is especially helpful when you are cutting and copying information between documents or applications.

Follow these steps to arrange your screen so that you can view multiple group windows:

1. Double-click the Accessories group icon to open the group windows. (The Main and Games windows should still be open from the preceding task; if not, open them.)

2. Move the Games window to the upper-left corner of the desktop, resizing the window if necessary.

3. Move the Main and Accessories group windows so that you can see the contents of all three group windows at once. (*Hint:* You may need to maximize the Program Manager window.)

Manually arranging group windows allows you to size the windows according to their importance and frequency of use.

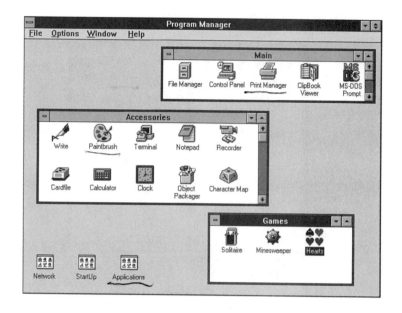

Task: Arrange Multiple Windows Automatically

Techniques discussed so far might be called "the manual way" of arranging windows. Windows also gives you two automatic methods: Tile and Cascade. These two methods are available in most Windows programs and apply to group, application, and document windows.

The Tile feature is located on the **W**indow menu in all Windows programs. Tile divides the application workspace evenly between the number of open group windows and then tiles the group windows from left to right on-screen. The Tile feature works well if you need to see only a small number of application icons in each group window.

Tile is a quick alternative to manually moving and sizing group windows so that you can see the contents of multiple windows.

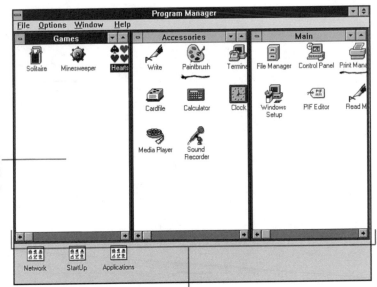

Windows are tiled from left to right and up and down

Each window is the same size

The Cascade feature also is located on the **W**indow menu. Cascade takes all open group windows, resizes them to the same size, and then creates an overlapping arrangement. Only the contents of one group window at a time can be seen.

Cascade is helpful if you work in multiple group windows, each with a large number of application icons.

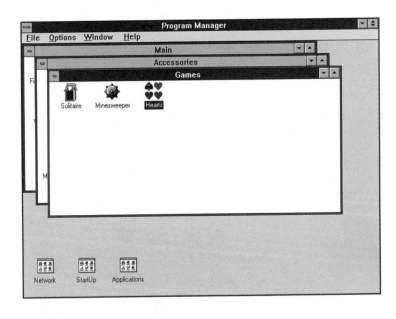

Lesson 4 covers the Tile and Cascade features in more detail.

Summary

To	Do This
Maximize a window	Click the Maximize button, or click the Control menu box and choose Ma**x**imize.
Restore a maximized window	Click the Restore button, or click the Control menu box and choose **R**estore.
Minimize a window	Click the Minimize button, or click the Control menu box and choose Mi**n**imize.
Restore a minimized window	Double-click the icon; or click the icon to open the Control menu, and then click **R**estore.
Resize a window	Move the mouse pointer over the window's border until the pointer changes to a double-headed arrow. Click and drag. Release the mouse button when you are finished resizing the window.
Use a scroll bar	Click the arrows on the vertical or horizontal scroll bar to move through a window. Click and drag the scroll box to move to a corner of the window. Click the area between the scroll box and one of the arrows on the scroll bar to move up or down in the window.
Move a window	Move the mouse pointer over the window's title bar. Click and drag. Release the mouse button when you are finished moving the window.

On Your Own
Estimated time: 15 minutes

1. If necessary, restore Program Manager to a window.

2. Maximize the Main group window in the Program Manager window.

3. Restore the Main group window.

4. Maximize the Program Manager window.

5. Resize the Accessories group window so that it's just big enough for all the program icons it contains.

6. Move the Games window to the lower-right corner of the application workspace.

7. Move and resize the rest of the program group windows to suit your computing habits. Remember that when you restore a window from an icon, the window is placed in its previous location.

Part II
Customizing Windows

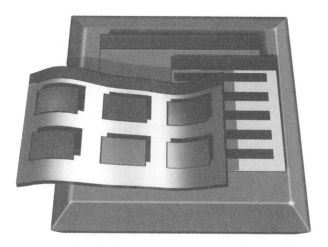

Lesson 3

Working with Groups and Applications

The Windows installation program creates the groups necessary to run Windows and its accompanying programs. During installation, Windows performs a search of your system for other installed applications and then sets them up for you in the Applications group. Although this is extremely helpful and gets you up and running right away, there may come a time when you want to create your own groups and set up other applications to customize Windows for your work habits.

In this lesson, you learn to

- Create new groups and program items

- Delete groups and program items

- Rename an icon

- Move and copy program icons between group windows

- Manually arrange program icons in a group

- Use Windows to arrange icons automatically

- Change the icon for a program item

Task: Add a New Group

During installation, Windows creates five program groups: Accessories, Games, Main, Applications, and StartUp. An additional group, called

Network, is created with Windows for Workgroups installation. You can continue to add your own program items to these groups, and you can create additional groups.

To create a new group, follow these steps:

1. Pull down the **F**ile menu.

2. Choose the **N**ew command. The New Program Object dialog box appears.

Use the New Program Object dialog box to create new groups and program items.

3. Click Program **G**roup.

4. Click OK. The Program Group Properties dialog box appears.

5. Type **Daily Business** in the **D**escription text box.

The description is usually something that describes the group.

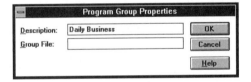

6. Click OK.

The Daily Business group window is created and positioned in the application workspace.

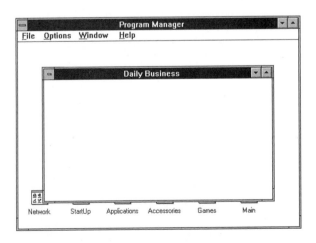

7. If you like, resize the Daily Business group window and move it to your preferred location in the Program Manager window.

Task: Add a Program Item to a Group

During a standard installation, Windows checks your system for program files and automatically creates program icons in the Applications group window. Many Windows programs create their own program groups and program items during installation. Other programs ask you to specify the group window to which you want to add the program item.

Program item icon
A small graphic image that represents a program installed on your system. This icon is also called an application icon.

You can easily create your own program items for both DOS and Windows programs. Because an icon is only a representation of the program, the same *program item icon* can appear in multiple windows. Furthermore, deleting a program item icon doesn't affect the program files.

Think of a program item icon as the ignition key to a car. The sole purpose of the key is to start the car; the purpose of the program item icon is to start the program. Just as you can have more than one key in more than one place, and any of those keys can start the car, you can have the same program item icon in more than one window, and any of those icons can start the program. If you move, lose, or destroy the key, you don't change the car in any way; moving, changing, or deleting the program item icon doesn't affect the program files on disk.

Note: *Microsoft recommends that you don't include more than 40 program items in a group. Instead, divide the program items among several program groups.*

For this example, add an icon for Windows Calculator to the Daily Business group window by following these steps:

1. Click anywhere in the Daily Business group window to make it the active window. (The active window's title bar appears in the same color as the Program Manager title bar.)

2. Pull down the **F**ile menu and choose **N**ew.

3. Click Program **I**tem.

4. Click OK.

The Program Item Properties dialog box contains the information necessary to set up an application.

5. The cursor is displayed in the Description text box. Type **Calculator**.

6. Click the **C**ommand Line text box to move the cursor down.

7. Click **B**rowse to open the Browse dialog box.

You use the Browse dialog box to locate the path (name and location) of a program file.

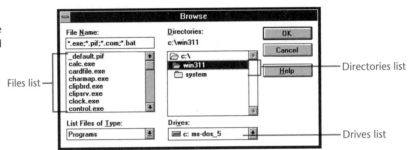

8. If necessary, select the Windows directory in the **D**irectories list. (You may have to use the scroll arrows to scroll through the list.)

9. Click calc.exe in the File **N**ame list box.

10. Click OK.

Browse inserts the full path of the program file into the **C**ommand Line text box.

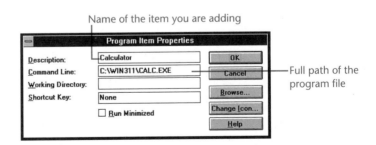

11. Click OK to create the program icon.

The Daily Business group window now contains a Calculator program icon.

If an icon is included with the program, it is displayed in the group window; otherwise, Windows assigns one of its generic icons to the program. Choosing another icon is covered later in this lesson.

If you have problems...

If you accidentally create a program item in the wrong group, don't delete it and start over! You can easily move that program's icon into the correct group window. See the task later in this lesson that covers moving and copying program icons between groups.

3

Task: Delete a Program Item

As your work habits change, you may want to delete program items from your group windows. Deleting a program icon doesn't affect the program files; remember that the icon is only a representation of the program.

To delete the Calculator program icon you just created, follow these steps:

1. Click the Calculator icon in the Daily Business group window.

2. Press Del.

   or

   Pull down the **F**ile menu and choose **D**elete.

You can confirm or cancel the deletion when the Delete dialog box appears.

3. Click the **Y**es command button to delete the Calculator program icon.

If you have problems...

If you have accidentally deleted the wrong program icon—don't panic—you have *not* deleted the program. As noted, a program icon is only a *representation* of the program. Use the steps listed in this section to re-create the program icon. Next time, read the confirmation message box carefully before responding.

Task: Delete a Group

If you create a group for a certain project, you might want to delete the group when you finish the project. When you delete a group, you also delete all the program icons in that group.

Follow these steps to delete the Daily Business group:

1. If necessary, click anywhere in the Daily Business group window to make the window active. (If a window is active, its title bar has the same color as the Program Manager title bar.)

2. Press Del.

   or

   Pull down the **F**ile menu and choose **D**elete.

   Note: *If you want to delete a group window that still has icons in it, you have to minimize the window first. Then select the group icon and press Del; or pull down the **F**ile menu and choose **D**elete.*

3. Click **Y**es in the Delete dialog box to confirm the deletion of the Daily Business group.

Caution
Make sure that the group you want to delete is the one listed in the confirmation message box. Re-creating a group can be a frustrating and time-consuming process.

Task: Rename an Icon

After you gain some experience with group and program icons, you may want to change the descriptions you assigned to them. When you update a program, for example, you may have to change the path for the file to start the program.

To change the description for the Solitaire program icon, follow these steps:

1. Open the Games group window.

2. Click the Solitaire program icon.

3. Pull down the **F**ile menu and choose **P**roperties.

The text in the **D**escription text box (Solitaire) is already selected, so you can type the new text in its place.

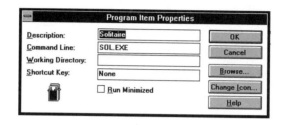

4. Type **Mouse Practice** in the **D**escription text box.

5. Click OK.

Now the Games group window is named Mouse Practice.

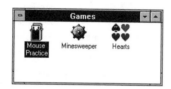

Follow these steps to change the description of the Games group window:

1. Minimize the Games group window.

2. Click the Games group icon.

3. Click the application workspace to cancel the Control menu. Alternatively, you can click the icon again.

4. Pull down the **F**ile menu and choose **P**roperties.

The text in the **D**escription text box (Games) is already selected, so you can type the new text in its place.

Program Group Properties		
Description:	Games	OK
Group File:	C:\WIN311\GAMES0.GRP	Cancel
		Help

3

5. Type **Mouse Practice Tools** in the **D**escription text box.

Notice the group file name specified in the Group **F**ile text box. When a group is created, Windows creates a group file with a GRP extension.

6. Click OK.

Now the description of the Games group is Mouse Practice Tools.

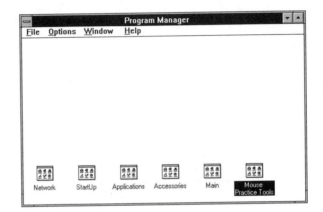

Task: Move and Copy Program Icons between Groups

As you become more familiar with Windows, you may want to organize your group windows differently. If you use one particular item frequently, for example, you might want to copy it into several group windows. Or you may decide that a program item is better suited to another group window.

Instead of re-creating the program items, you can move and copy program items between group windows. Although the **F**ile menu contains options that move and copy program items, you can also use the mouse "drag and drop" method. This is the fastest and easiest method.

To move the Calculator program icon from the Accessories group window to the Applications group window, follow these steps:

1. Open the Accessories and Applications group windows.

2. Click the Calculator program icon in the Accessories group window.

3. Hold down the mouse button and drag the icon to the Applications group window.

Note: *If you drag the program icon across the application workspace to the other group window, the black-and-white icon changes to the international "no" symbol—a circle with a line through it. This symbol means that you can't drop the program icon in the application workspace.*

A black-and-white icon (without the description) appears as you drag the mouse.

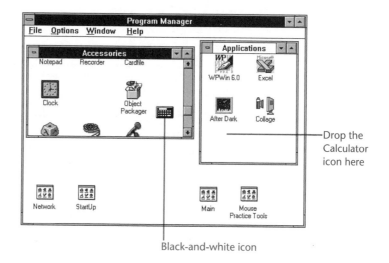

Drop the Calculator icon here

Black-and-white icon

4. Release the mouse button to drop the Calculator program icon into position.

The Calculator icon now appears in the Applications group window.

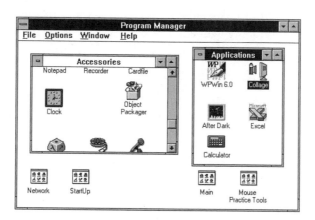

If you use a certain program item frequently, it might be easier to have it in multiple group windows.

To copy the Clock program icon to the Applications group window, follow these steps:

1. Click the Clock program icon in the Accessories group window.

2. Hold down the Ctrl key.

3. Click and drag the icon to the Applications group window.

4. Release the mouse button and the Ctrl key to drop the icon into position.

If you have problems...

If you accidentally drop an icon in the wrong group, just pick up the icon again and drag it to the intended location. After you drop an icon into position, the other icons may move over to accommodate the new icon. In this case, the Auto Arrange feature is turned on, and Windows is trying to help you avoid overlapping your icons. Auto Arrange is discussed in the next section.

Task: Arrange Items in a Group

The preceding lesson discussed moving group windows in the application workspace. You can move and size windows manually or automatically (by using commands in the **W**indow menu). You can use similar methods to arrange the application icons within group windows. Positioning frequently used application icons in the upper-left corner of the group window makes them easier to find.

Note: *If you are adjusting icon placement and the icons seem to jump around on their own or behave in unexpected ways, the Auto Arrange feature is probably turned on. This feature is explained a little later in this lesson.*

You can arrange the application icons (or program items) inside a group window by clicking and dragging the icons to new locations. The Auto Arrange feature makes sure that you don't drag icons on top of each other, possibly hiding an important icon. You can also choose the **Ar**range Icons menu command and have Windows arrange the icons in the group window for you.

Follow these steps to arrange program icons within the Applications group window:

1. Open the Applications group window.

2. Place the mouse pointer on the icon or the icon description.

3. Click and drag the icon to a new place in the Applications group window.

Rearrange the program icons so that the programs you use most often are easy to find.

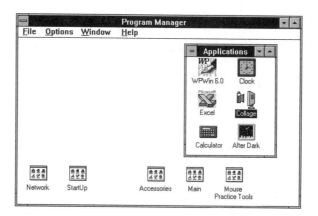

If you have problems...

If you accidentally make a mess while arranging icons, you can exit Windows without saving your changes and then start over. Pull down the **O**ptions menu. If **S**ave Settings on Exit has a check mark beside it, it is currently turned on, and your changes will be saved when you exit Windows. Click **S**ave Settings on Exit to turn off the option. Now exit Windows and then restart Windows to go back to your previous arrangement.

Note: *You may want to maximize the group window to make rearranging the program icons easier.*

As noted, the Auto Arrange feature prevents icons from overlapping. When you drag and drop an icon to a new location, Auto Arrange automatically moves the existing icon to accommodate the insertion.

Follow these steps to turn on Auto Arrange:

1. Pull down the **O**ptions menu.

2. If a check mark appears next to **A**uto Arrange, the feature is already turned on. Click anywhere outside the menu to cancel the menu.

   or

   If you don't see a check mark, choose **A**uto Arrange to turn on the feature.

When you turn on Auto Arrange, Windows places a check mark next to the menu command.

Check mark ⎯

Click here to cancel ⎯ the menu

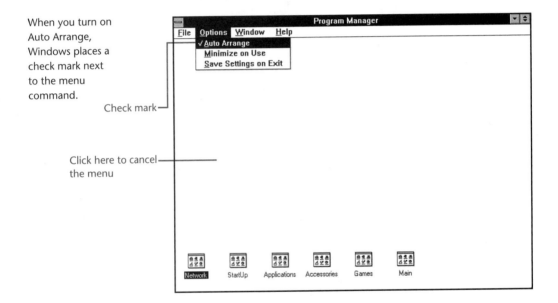

Note: *One advantage of manually arranging program icons in a group window is that you can place your icons closer together than Auto Arrange allows. Another is that Windows doesn't try to "help" you by moving other icons that are already where you want them!*

You can use the **A**rrange Icons command to arrange icons, evenly spaced, in group windows. You can use this command also in the Program Manager window to place the group icons at the bottom of the application workspace.

To automatically arrange the program icons in a group window, follow these steps:

1. Click the title bar of the group window to select it.

In this example, the icons are scattered around in the group window.

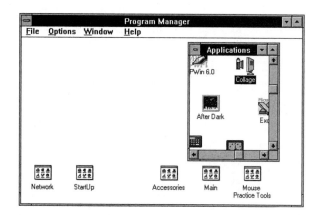

2. Pull down the **W**indow menu and choose **A**rrange Icons.

The **A**rrange Icons command positions the program icons evenly spaced in the group window.

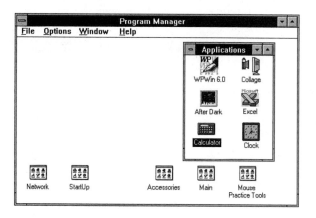

Notice how the scroll bars will disappear when you get the arrangement right, thus clearing up the screen clutter.

To automatically arrange the group icons in the Program Manager window, follow these steps:

1. Click a group icon.

In this example, the group icons are scattered around in the Program Manager window.

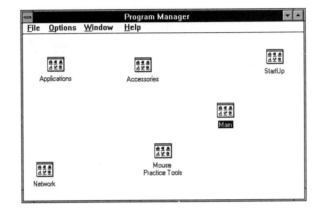

2. Click the icon again to clear the Control menu.

3. Pull down the **W**indow menu and choose **A**rrange Icons.

The **A**rrange Icons command places the group icons at the bottom of the Program Manager window.

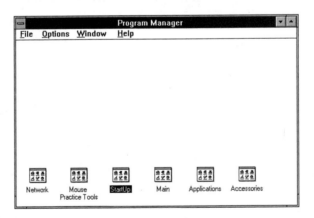

If you have problems...

If you accidentally make a mess while arranging icons, you can exit Windows without saving your changes and then start over. Pull down the **O**ptions menu. If **S**ave Settings on Exit has a check mark next to it, that option is currently turned on, and your changes will be saved when you exit Windows. Choose **S**ave Settings on Exit to turn it off. Now exit Windows and then re-start it to go back to your previous arrangement.

Task: Change an Icon

Most Windows programs come with their own icons, which graphically represent the type of program. Most DOS programs, however, don't come with icons for the Windows desktop. If the program doesn't have an icon available, Windows uses a standard icon. The standard icons are not very descriptive of the type of program.

If you want to change the icon assigned to a program item, there are two files included with the Windows program that contain a series of icons. Third-party manufacturers also produce packages of icons that can be used in Windows. In fact, programs that enable you to create and edit your own icons are available.

Follow these steps to change the icon for the Solitaire program:

1. Open the Mouse Practice Tools (Games) group window.

2. Click the Mouse Practice (Solitaire) icon.

3. Pull down the **F**ile menu and choose **P**roperties.

Note: *Alternatively, you can press Alt+Enter to display the properties for a selected program item.*

The Program Item Properties dialog box appears, with the current icon displayed in the lower-left corner.

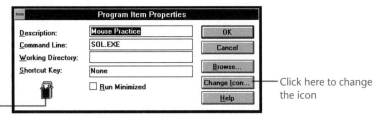

Current icon

Click here to change the icon

4. Click Change **I**con.

5. Type **progman.exe** in the File **N**ame text box. Because the text was already selected, your typing replaced the existing text.

All the icons in the PROGMAN.EXE file are displayed in the **Cur**rent Icon box.

Note: *Another Windows file also contains icons. The name of this file is MORICONS.DLL.*

6. Click the scroll arrows to move through the list; then click the Mona Lisa icon.

7. Click OK.

The new icon is
displayed in the
lower-left corner of
the dialog box.

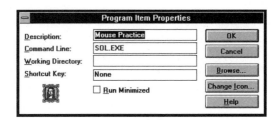

8. Click OK to change the icon.

Summary

To	Do This
Add a new group	Pull down the **F**ile menu and choose **N**ew. Click Program **G**roup and then click OK. Type the name of the group in the **D**escription text box. Click OK. Move and size the new group window as needed.
Add a program item to a group	Pull down the **F**ile menu and choose **N**ew. Click Program **I**tem and then click OK. Type the name of the program in the **D**escription text box. Click **C**ommand Line. Type the full path of the program name; or click **B**rowse, specify the program file, and click OK. Click OK to add the program item.
Delete a program icon	Click the program icon. Press Del, or pull down the **F**ile menu and choose **D**elete. Click **Y**es in the Delete dialog box to confirm the deletion.
Delete an empty group window	Click the group icon. Press Del, or pull down the **F**ile menu and choose **D**elete. Verify the correct group name and then click **Y**es in the Delete dialog box to confirm the deletion.
Delete a group window containing program icons	Minimize the group window. Click the group icon. Press Del, or pull down the **F**ile menu and choose **D**elete. Verify the correct group name and then click **Y**es in the Delete dialog box to confirm the deletion.

To	Do This
Rename an icon	Click the icon. Pull down the **F**ile menu and choose **P**roperties, or press Alt+Enter. Type a new name in the **D**escription text box. Click OK.
Move and copy program icons between groups	Open the group windows. Click the program item to move or copy. To copy the icon, hold down Ctrl and drag the icon to the new location. To move the icon, just drag the icon to the new location. Release the mouse button to drop the icon into position.
Arrange program items	Click and drag the icon to a new location. Release the mouse button to drop the icon into position.
Turn on Auto Arrange	Pull down the **O**ptions menu. If a check mark appears next to **A**uto Arrange, the feature is already turned on. Otherwise, choose the **A**uto Arrange command.
Automatically arrange icons in a group window	Click the title bar of the group window. Pull down the **W**indow menu and choose **A**rrange Icons.
Automatically arrange group icons in Program Manager	Click a group icon. Click the icon again to clear the Control menu. Pull down the **W**indow menu and choose **A**rrange Icons.
Change to a different icon	Click the program icon. Pull down the **F**ile menu and choose **P**roperties, or press Alt+Enter. Click Change **I**con. Type the name of the file containing the icons (PROGMAN.EXE or MORICONS.DLL). Click the icon you want; then click OK twice.

On Your Own
Estimated time: 20 minutes

1. Turn off the Auto Arrange feature. Click and drag icons on top of each other. Turn on the Auto Arrange feature and watch the icons line up.

2. Click and drag the group icons around in the application workspace to scatter them on-screen. Use the Arrange Icons feature to line up the icons at the bottom of the screen.

3. Arrange the program icons in the Main group window so that the File Manager and Print Manager icons are in the upper-left corner.

4. Create a group window with your name as the description.

5. Add a program item for the Clock application (CLOCK.EXE) to your new group window.

6. Copy the File Manager, Print Manager, and Solitaire icons to your group window.

7. Change the icon for Solitaire to one of your choice. Use either PROGMAN.EXE or MORICONS.DLL to make your selection.

8. Delete the program icons from your group window.

9. Delete your group window.

10. Change the icon for the Mouse Practice (Solitaire) game back to the original icon. *(Hint:* Type **sol.exe** as the name of the file containing the Solitaire icon.)

11. Rename the Mouse Practice program icon back to Solitaire, and the Mouse Practice Tools group window back to Games.

Starting and Controlling Applications

One of the advantages of Windows is that it enables you to start and run multiple applications at the same time. Switching between programs increases productivity and facilitates the sharing of information among applications.

This lesson covers starting applications, switching between applications, and arranging program windows. Specifically, you learn to

- Start applications
- Close program windows
- Switch between programs
- Tile and cascade windows
- Start programs automatically when you start Windows
- Get to a DOS prompt without exiting Windows
- Open a window for the DOS prompt

Task: Start an Application

Starting applications in Windows is much easier than in DOS. To start an application in DOS, you have to type the exact command to start the program, and you may have to know exactly where the program is located on your system. In Windows, an application is represented by an icon on the desktop. All you have to do to start a program is select the program's icon.

To start the Calculator program, follow these steps:

1. Open the Accessories group window.

   Note: *If you completed the task in Lesson 3 to move the Calculator program icon to the Applications group window, look in that group window instead.*

2. Locate the Calculator program icon. You may have to use the scroll arrows to move through the window.

3. Double-click the Calculator icon to start the Calculator program.

You use the Calculator program to compute basic calculations.

Most programs are opened in a window, which you can move, size, and arrange with the same methods used for group windows. The Calculator program is opened in a small window that can be moved and arranged, but not sized. Note the very thin border around the window. A thin border indicates that a window cannot be sized.

Caution

Closing a program window is different from minimizing the window. Minimizing shrinks the window to an icon but doesn't exit the program.

Task: Close a Window with the Control Menu

To close a program window, you have to exit the program. Most Windows applications have an **Exit** command on the **F**ile menu. Other programs have their own methods for exiting.

The Calculator window is a special case. It doesn't have a File option on the menu bar, so no Exit command is available. To close Calculator, you have to use the Control menu or the Task List (discussed later in this lesson).

Follow these steps to use the Control menu to close the Calculator window:

1. Click the Control menu box in the Calculator window.

2. Choose **C**lose.

There are two types of Control menus: application and document. An application Control menu controls the application; a document Control menu controls the document. The application Control menu box that opens the Control menu is found in the application's title bar. The line in that Control menu box resembles a space bar; thus, the keyboard shortcut for opening an application Control menu is Alt+space bar. The line in the document Control menu resembles a hyphen (or dash), so the keyboard shortcut for opening the document Control menu is Alt+–.

Double-click the application Control menu box in Program Manager to exit Windows.

Application Control menu box

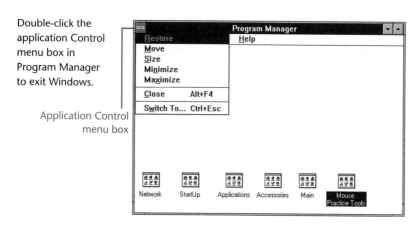

Double-click the document Control menu box in the Accessories group window to close or minimize the window.

Document Control menu box

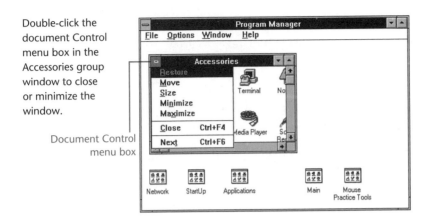

Clicking a Control menu box opens the Control menu where you can make a selection. Double-clicking a Control menu box automatically closes the window (application or group) or the document. The options on the Control menus are essentially the same. Additional options may be offered depending on the menu's location in an application, group window, or document.

Working with Multiple Application Windows

You can run multiple applications at the same time in Windows. How many programs you can run depends on how much memory you have on your system. Each application is run in a window, and like a window, can be manipulated on the desktop.

Note: *Minimizing an application does not reduce the amount of memory consumed by the program.*

If you need to run a large number of programs at the same time, it's easier to minimize all the program windows to icons on the desktop. Then all you have to do is double-click the program icon to open the window. When you are finished, you just minimize the window to an icon again.

You can reduce Program Manager to an icon (as shown in the next figure) or a window. If Program Manager is reduced to a window, minimized program icons will appear below the Program Manager window.

All program
windows, including
Program Manager,
are reduced to icons
on the desktop.

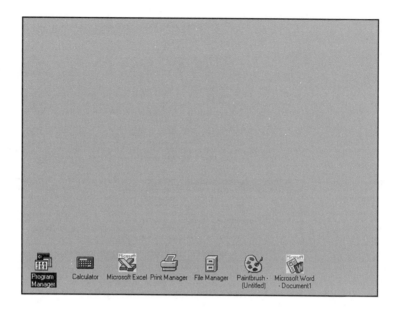

4

Depending on the project, you may want to maximize program windows
so that only one program window is displayed at a time. By maximizing
the window, you can see more of the program.

The Paintbrush
program is used to
create and edit
graphic images.

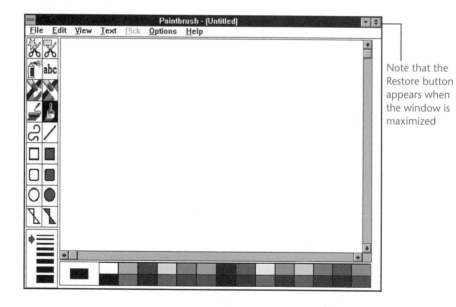

Note that the
Restore button
appears when
the window is
maximized

Finally, if you are sharing information among programs, it might be
helpful to see all the program windows at once. You can size and move

the windows manually, or you can arrange the open windows by using commands on the Task List, as described in the next section.

Task: Switch between Programs

The Task List is a dialog box with a list of programs that are currently running. You can use Task List options to arrange open windows, close windows, and arrange icons. The Task List is extremely helpful when your program windows overlap and you "lose" program windows.

The Task List's Tile feature automatically arranges program windows for you.

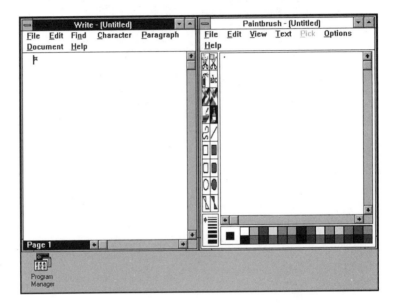

The Task List displays a list of all open programs, including Program Manager. You can switch to another program by selecting the program name in the list.

To switch between programs with the Task List, follow these steps:

1. Start the Paintbrush program (in the Accessories group).

2. Minimize Paintbrush. This moves the window out of the way so that you can start another program from Program Manager.

3. Start the Write program (also in the Accessories group).

4. Click the Control menu box in the Write window and choose Switch To.

Always check the
Task List before
starting a program;
you may be
accidentally starting
a second copy.

Click here to close the
selected program window

Click here to switch to the selected program

> **Note:** *Alternatively, you can press Ctrl+Esc to display the Task List, or you can double-click the desktop.*

5. Select Paintbrush in the Task list and then choose **S**witch To.

   or

   Double-click Paintbrush in the Task List.

You can use two shortcuts to switch from one application to another: Alt+Tab and Alt+Esc. To cycle among open applications, hold down the Alt key and then press and release Tab or Esc. Release both keys when you find the application you want. The difference between the shortcuts is that Alt+Tab displays a small dialog box in the middle of the current window with the name of the application you will switch to when you release the keys; Alt+Esc actually displays the applications as you move through them.

Task: Tile Program Windows

The Tile feature in the Task List divides the application workspace evenly among the open programs and then tiles the program windows, from left to right, on-screen. The Tile feature works well if you need to see only a small portion of each program window.

Note: *The **T**ile and **C**ascade commands in the Task List permanently resize your application windows. If you want them positioned and sized as you had them before the tile or cascade operation, you will have to do that manually.*

Follow these steps to tile the Paintbrush and Write programs:

1. Click the Control menu box in the Paintbrush window and choose S**w**itch To.

2. Click **T**ile.

Program Manager is considered to be a program window as well, so it is included when you tile program windows (unless Program Manager is minimized).

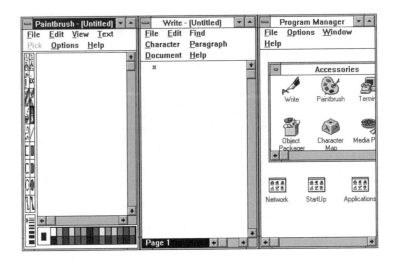

3. Minimize Program Manager.

4. Click the Control menu box in the Paintbrush window and choose S**w**itch To.

5. Click **T**ile.

Now only two windows are tiled: Write and Paintbrush. Notice how the menus in a tiled application wrap down to a second or third line so that all the menu commands are still visible in the smaller window.

Active window
The window in which you are currently working.

To work in a program window, you must make the program window *active*. Click in the title bar or anywhere in the window where you want to work. The color of the title bar for an active window is different from the color of the title bar for an inactive window.

If you have problems...

Tiling the Program Manager window reduces the size of the window and may cause program items to disappear. Use the scroll bars to move through the window until you see the items you need.

Task: Cascade Program Windows

The Cascade feature in the Task List takes all the open program windows, resizes them to the same size, and then overlaps them. Cascade creates a nice arrangement of title bars that you can click to switch among windows. Only the contents of one group window can be seen at a time.

To cascade the Paintbrush and Write programs, follow these steps:

1. Click the Control menu box in the Paintbrush window.

2. Choose **Sw**itch To.

3. Click **C**ascade.

Cascade is helpful when you have several program windows to arrange.

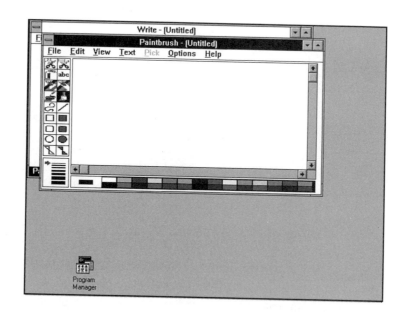

To switch between cascaded windows, click anywhere in the window you want to make active. Remember that the title bar of the active window appears in a different color.

If you have problems...

Cascading may create multiple layers of cascaded windows, making the window you want to use even harder to find. You may find it necessary to click and drag a window out of the way to get to the other windows.

Task: Close a Program Window with the Task List

You can use the Task List to close program windows. Before going on, use the Task List to close the Paintbrush and Write program windows. Follow these steps:

1. Click the Control menu box in the Paintbrush window.

2. Choose **Sw**itch To.

3. Select Paintbrush from the list.

4. Click **E**nd Task.

   Note: *If you have made changes to a document in a program, Windows will open the program window and prompt you to save the changes.*

5. Click the Control menu box in the Write window.

6. Choose S**w**itch To.

7. Select Write from the list.

8. Click **E**nd Task.

9. If necessary, close any other active program windows until Program Manager is the last item on the list.

   Note: *If you click **E**nd Task when Program Manager is selected in the Task List, you will exit the Windows program.*

Task: Set Up the StartUp Group

The StartUp group is created during Windows installation, or you can create your own StartUp group later. Programs in this group are started automatically when you start the Windows program. If you copy program icons into the StartUp group, Windows will start each program, in turn, for you. The changes take effect the next time you start Windows.

Think about the programs you use every day and consider placing their program icons in the StartUp group. An accountant might want 1-2-3 for Windows and the Calculator program. Writers might want WordPerfect for Windows and a screen-capture program. Network administrators might want NetWatcher and WinMeter for monitoring the system.

Follow these steps to create the StartUp group:

1. Switch to Program Manager.

2. Pull down the **F**ile menu and choose **N**ew.

3. Click Program **G**roup and then click OK. The Program Group Properties dialog box appears.

4. Type **StartUp** in the **D**escription text box.

5. Click OK.

6. Move and size the StartUp window as necessary.

Refer to Lesson 3, "Working with Groups and Applications," for the steps to move and copy program icons into your new StartUp group.

Working in DOS from Windows

At times, you may need to execute a DOS command but don't want to exit Windows. The MS-DOS Prompt program icon in the Main group window opens a DOS "window" where you can type DOS commands. You should reserve the use of this feature for little tasks that are not done efficiently with other Windows features, such as File Manager.

Some DOS commands will not work properly while Windows is running. Two examples are the CHKDSK and SCANDISK commands. You should also avoid using disk-optimization programs while Windows is running.

You may run out of memory if you try to run a large application from the DOS prompt, because Windows takes up a large portion of available memory. If the DOS command cannot be completed successfully, the system may crash, and you will lose any data you did not previously save while in Windows.

You can run a popular DOS program, MS-DOS Editor, from the DOS prompt. DOS 5 and later versions include the Editor program, which you can use to open and edit system files, such as AUTOEXEC.BAT and CONFIG.SYS, as well as any other batch files you have on your system. To run Editor, type **edit** at the DOS prompt.

Task: Access the DOS Prompt

Disk operating system (DOS)
Acts as an interpreter between you and your computer, translating your commands into computer language.

The Main group has a program item called MS-DOS. This item opens a "window" to the *disk operating system (DOS)*, enabling you to issue DOS commands without leaving Windows.

Follow these steps to open a DOS screen and issue a DOS command:

1. Open the Main group window if it is not already open.

4

2. Locate the MS-DOS program item. Use the scroll arrows if necessary to scroll through the group window.

3. Double-click the MS-DOS program icon.

The MS-DOS information is displayed at the top of the screen.

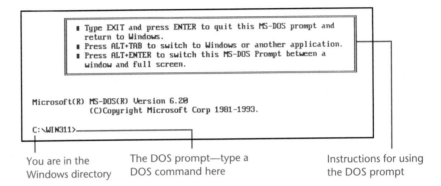

- Type EXIT and press ENTER to quit this MS-DOS prompt and return to Windows.
- Press ALT+TAB to switch to Windows or another application.
- Press ALT+ENTER to switch this MS-DOS Prompt between a window and full screen.

Microsoft(R) MS-DOS(R) Version 6.20
          (C)Copyright Microsoft Corp 1981-1993.

C:\WIN311>

You are in the Windows directory

The DOS prompt—type a DOS command here

Instructions for using the DOS prompt

4. Type **dir** to get a directory and file listing in the Windows directory.

5. Type **exit**.

6. Press Enter to close the MS-DOS screen and return to Program Manager.

Task: Display the DOS Prompt in a Window

If you prefer, you can reduce the MS-DOS screen to a window, which takes up less space.

Follow these steps to open a window for the DOS prompt:

1. Open the Main group window.

2. Double-click the MS-DOS program icon.

3. Press Alt+Enter.

The MS-DOS screen is now a small window in Program Manager.

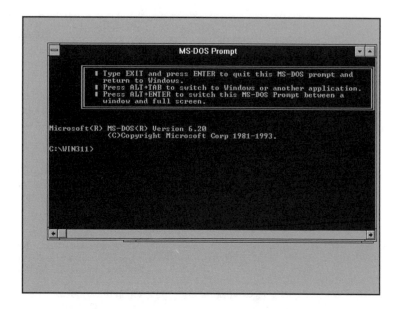

Note the Minimize and Maximize buttons. Use them to reduce the window to an icon or expand it to the full width of the screen.

4. To switch back to a full screen, press Alt+Enter again.

5. To exit DOS and return to Windows, type **exit** at the DOS prompt and press Enter.

Summary

To	Do This
Start an application	Double-click the program icon.
Close an application	Use the appropriate steps to exit the program, or pull down the **F**ile menu and choose E**x**it. If a **F**ile menu is not available, click the Control menu box and choose **C**lose.
Open the Task List	Press Ctrl+Esc, double-click the desktop, or click the application Control menu box and choose S**w**itch To.
Switch between programs	Open the Task List. Double-click the program name, or select the program name and choose S**w**itch To.

(continues)

To	Do This
Tile multiple programs	Start the applications. Open the Task List and click **T**ile. To switch between tiled windows, click anywhere in the window you want to make active.
Cascade multiple programs	Start the applications. Open the Task List and click **C**ascade. To switch between cascaded windows, click anywhere in the window you want to make active.
Start programs automatically when you start windows	Copy or move the program icons into the StartUp group. The next time you start Windows, those programs will be started automatically.
Open a DOS screen	Open the Main group window. Double-click the MS-DOS program icon. Type the DOS command you want to use. Type **exit** and press Enter to go back to Windows.
Open a window for the DOS prompt	Open the Main group window. Double-click the MS-DOS program icon. Press Alt+Enter. Type exit and press Enter to close the window and return to Windows.

On Your Own
Estimated time: 20 minutes

1. Start an application and then use the Control menu to close it.

2. Open several program windows and practice using the Task List to Switch among the programs.

3. Use the shortcut keys to switch among the programs.

4. Use the Task List to close the program windows.

5. Access the MS-DOS prompt and get a directory listing of files.

6. Open a window for MS-DOS.

7. Switch between a window and a full screen for MS-DOS.

8. Exit the DOS window.

9. *Optional*: Copy the program icon of your choice into the StartUp group.

Lesson 5

Personalizing Windows

With Control Panel, you can customize Windows in many ways to suit your needs. You can change the colors used in windows, title bars, dialog boxes, and so on. The background can be changed to a color, pattern, or picture. A screen saver is available to help prevent monitor "burn in." You can fine-tune the mouse response and even swap the buttons if you are left-handed. When you need to reset the system clock, you can do it in Windows. You can turn sounds on and off, and you can assign sounds to system events.

The changes you make in Control Panel will affect only *your* Windows setup, even if you are on a network. Your changes will go into effect immediately and remain in effect even after you exit Windows.

This lesson shows you how to

- Change the screen colors

- Customize a color scheme

- Assign a pattern or wallpaper to the desktop

- Turn on the Screen Saver utility

- Adjust the system date and time

- Enable fast switching between programs

- Adjust the speed and sensitivity of the mouse

- Swap the left and right mouse buttons

- Turn off system sounds

- Assign a sound to an event

Using Control Panel

Control Panel is a program item icon within the Main group window of Program Manager. The tools contained in Control Panel enable you to customize many features in Windows.

To open Control Panel, open the Main group window and double-click the Control Panel icon.

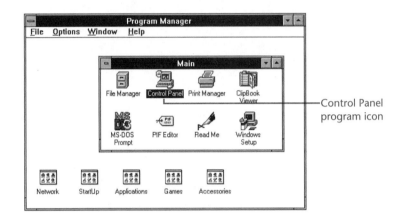

Control Panel program icon

Each icon within the Control Panel window represents a program you can use to customize a Windows feature.

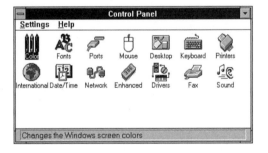

The 386 Enhanced icon is displayed only when you are running in 386 Enhanced mode. You will see a Network icon if you are connected to a network, and an ODBC icon if you have ODBC data source drivers installed on your system. Finally, the Fax icon appears only if you have the Windows for Workgroups Add-On installed.

Note: *Depending on how your system is configured and any additional equipment you are using, you may see additional icons, or your icons may appear slightly different from those shown in this section.*

Table 5.1 lists the Control Panel tools and describes their purposes.

Table 5.1 Control Panel Tools

Tool	Icon	Description
Color		Changes the colors in the desktop and parts of windows.
Fonts		Adds or removes printer fonts, screen fonts, and TrueType fonts.
Ports		Defines your serial communication ports.
Mouse		Adjusts mouse speed, sensitivity, and left or right button control; also sets mouse trails. (Depending on the type of mouse you use, your options may differ.)
Desktop		Changes the patterns or pictures on the desktop background.
Keyboard		Changes the keyboard's rate of repeating.
Printers		Adds or removes printers, configures printers, and sets the default printer.
International		Changes the display for different languages, dates, times, and currencies.
Date/Time		Resets the computer's date and time.
Network		Specifies workstation and workgroup names and options for startup, password, and event logs. (This icon appears only if you are attached to a network; depending on your network setup, you may have different options.)
ODBC		Adds, modifies, or deletes ODBC drivers and data sources. (This icon appears only if you have ODBC drivers on your system.)
Sound		Assigns sounds to events and turns sound on and off.
386 Enhanced		Indicates how programs share the power when Windows is in 386 Enhanced mode. (This icon appears only when you are running in 386 Enhanced mode.)
Drivers		Installs and configures drivers for peripherals such as sound boards and pen tablets.
Fax		Selects EMail and Fax capabilities, or just Fax. (This icon appears only if you have Windows for Workgroups installed.)

5

To start a Control Panel program, double-click the program icon. As an alternative, you can open the **S**ettings menu and select from a list the program you want to start.

Changing the Screen Colors

You can customize the color schemes that define colors for window elements. The colors you use can make working with Windows programs more enjoyable than working with monochrome DOS programs. You can also design color schemes to help reduce eye strain.

Task: Select a Color Scheme

Color scheme

A set of colors for Windows backgrounds, title bars, window borders, menus, and other elements.

Windows comes with a list of predefined *color schemes* that determine the colors of your windows, desktop, and screen elements. You can use these schemes or create your own.

To change your screen colors to one of the predefined color schemes, follow these steps:

1. Double-click the Color icon in Control Panel.

2. Click the underlined down arrow at the right side of the Color **S**chemes list box.

3. Click Cinnamon from the drop-down list. Notice the color changes shown in the sample screen.

The sample screen in the dialog box shows how the various parts of the windows will appear with these colors.

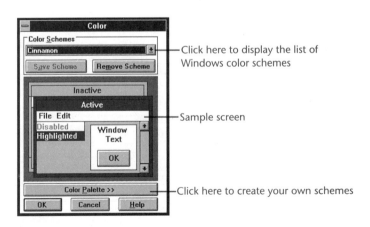

4. Click the underlined down arrow at the right side of the Color **S**chemes list box to redisplay the list of color schemes.

5. Scroll down through the list and click The Blues.

   Note: *While the drop-down list is selected, you can instead type a letter to change to the color scheme that begins with that letter. For example, type **T** to change to The Blues.*

6. Select a color scheme that is pleasing to you, or select Windows Default (at the top of the list) to return to the default color scheme.

7. Click OK to save your changes.

If you have problems...

If you don't like the new color scheme, click Cancel. Your changes will not be saved, and the scheme will revert back to the original selection.

Task: Customize a Color Scheme

You can create your own color scheme by modifying one of the pre-defined schemes that comes with Windows. New color schemes can be saved and added to the list of predefined schemes.

Follow these steps to customize a color scheme:

1. Double-click the Color icon in Control Panel.

2. Click the underlined down arrow at the right side of the Color **S**chemes list box.

3. Click the name of the scheme that most closely resembles the colors you want.

4. Click Color **P**alette. The dialog box expands to show the palette of colors from which you can choose.

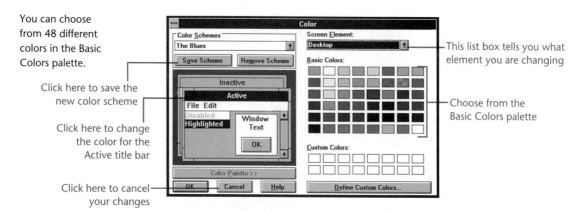

You can choose from 48 different colors in the Basic Colors palette.

Click here to save the new color scheme

Click here to change the color for the Active title bar

Click here to cancel your changes

This list box tells you what element you are changing

Choose from the Basic Colors palette

5. Click the part of the sample window that you want to change—in this case, the Active title bar. Alternatively, you can select the element from the Screen **E**lement list box.

6. Click the color you want from the **B**asic Colors palette. A dark border appears around the selected color, and the title bar in the sample changes to the new color.

   Note: *Up to 16 custom colors can be created for use in color schemes. Refer to Que's* Using Windows, *3.11 Edition, Special Edition, for a complete discussion.*

7. Click S**a**ve Scheme.

8. In the Save Scheme dialog box, type your name in the text box.

9. Click OK to add your new color scheme to the list.

If you have problems... If you don't like the changes you have made to a color scheme, just click Cancel. Your changes will not be saved, and the colors will revert back to the original scheme.

Customizing the Desktop

Desktop

In addition to changing the colors of your windows, you can change the pattern or wallpaper of the desktop behind the windows. The desktop behind windows and icons can have a color, selected from the Color dialog box; a pattern, selected from the Desktop dialog box; or a wallpaper, selected from the Desktop dialog box.

Pattern
A pattern that appears across your desktop. You can create your own pattern or select one of the patterns included with Windows.

Task: Select a Desktop Pattern

Your desktop—the part of your screen outside all windows—doesn't have to be a solid color or shade. Instead, you can decorate it with a *pattern*. Windows comes with predefined patterns you can select, or you can create your own. The color of the pattern is the same as the color for window text (usually black), which you define in the Color dialog box.

To choose a desktop pattern, follow these steps:

1. Double-click the Desktop icon in Control Panel.

The Desktop dialog
box appears.

2. To open the drop-down list of patterns, click the underlined down
arrow next to **N**ame in the Pattern section of the dialog box.

3. Scroll through the list to see the patterns that are included with
Windows.

4. Click the underlined down arrow again to close the drop-down list.

5. Click Edit **P**attern to open the Edit Pattern dialog box.

6. Click the underlined down arrow next to the **N**ame text box to
display the list of patterns.

7. Click the Diamonds pattern.

The Edit Pattern
dialog box displays
a sample of the
pattern as it will
appear on the
desktop, as well as a
close-up so that you
can see the details.

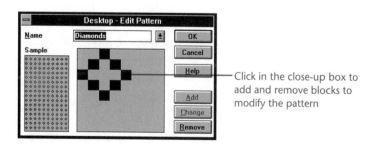

Click in the close-up box to
add and remove blocks to
modify the pattern

8. Click OK to add the pattern to the desktop.

The diamond
pattern now covers
the entire desktop
area.

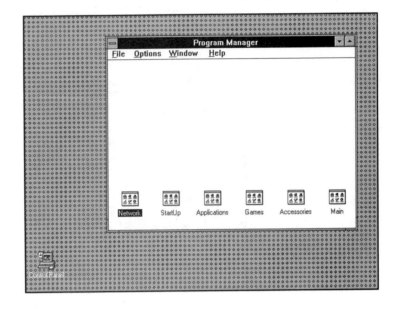

Note: *If you want to remove a pattern from your desktop, select the (None) option from the top of the drop-down list.*

Task: Select a Wallpaper

Wallpaper
The bit-mapped
(BMP) drawing
used as a backdrop
behind windows on
the desktop.

You can customize the desktop so that it displays a picture or graphic, called *wallpaper*. For the desktop wallpaper, you can use the drawings that come with Windows, create your own drawings with Windows Paintbrush or other graphics programs, or scan photographs with a scanner.

Wallpaper uses files stored in bit-mapped format, with a BMP extension. To use these files as wallpaper, you can either store them in the Windows directory or specify the correct path and name of the file when selecting the wallpaper.

Note: *Using wallpaper for a desktop background takes up more memory than a plain background. If your computer is low on memory, don't use a wallpaper desktop.*

To display a wallpaper as the desktop background, follow these steps:

1. Double-click the Desktop icon in Control Panel.

2. Click the underlined down arrow next to the Wallpaper **F**ile list box to display a list of the wallpaper files in the Windows directory.

3. Click the name of the wallpaper you want to use. For this example, select arcade.bmp from the list.

If you have problems...

If you have selected a pattern *and* wallpaper, the pattern appears behind the names of program icons. If the pattern makes the names hard to read, select (None) from the Pattern **N**ame list.

---

4. Click **T**ile to fill the desktop with the image. The **T**ile option uses multiple images to fill the background.

or

Click **C**enter so that the surrounding desktop displays the selected color or pattern if the image isn't large enough to fill the desktop.

5. Click OK to use the wallpaper.

The ARCADE.BMP file (tiled) produces an interesting background that covers the desktop area.

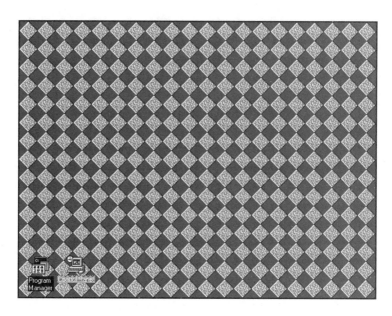

5

The WINLOGO.BMP file is centered on the Diamonds desktop pattern.

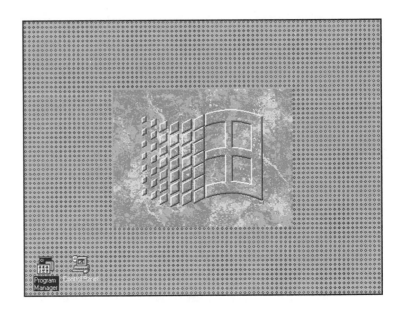

Note: *If you want to remove a wallpaper from your desktop, select the (None) option from the top of the drop-down list.*

Task: Turn On the Screen Saver

Screen saver
A program that replaces the screen image with a moving pattern when the computer is idle.

The *Screen Saver* feature replaces your screen image with a moving pattern when you haven't used your computer within a specified time period—thus helping to prevent an image from "burning into" your computer screen. Pressing any key or using the mouse restores the desktop to the screen. Several screen saver images are included with Windows 3.11.

To turn on Screen Saver, follow these steps:

1. Double-click the Desktop icon in Control Panel.

2. Select a screen saver from the Screen Saver N**a**me drop-down list. For example, click Starfield Simulation.

3. Click T**e**st to see how the screen saver will look.

4. Move the mouse when you are ready to stop the test.

5. Now select the Marquee screen saver from the Screen Saver N**a**me list.

6. Click the Set**u**p button to specify other parameters for the screen saver. (The Blank Screen option has no setup parameters.)

Some screen savers, such as Marquee, have different parameters that you can set up.

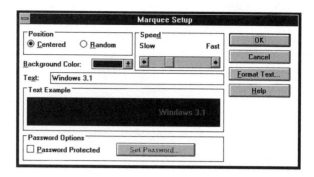

7. To change the marquee text, type the new text in the Text text box. For this example, type **Don't go away - I'll be right back!**

8. Click **R**andom to have the text appear at random locations on-screen, or click **C**entered if you want the marquee to crawl across the center of the screen.

9. If you like, click **F**ormat Text and change the font and size of the text. You can also change the speed of the marquee's crawl by adjusting the Spee**d** scroll box.

10. Click OK.

11. Click T**e**st to see how the screen saver will look.

The new marquee text crawls across the screen at random locations.

Delay time
The number of
minutes that pass
before the screen
saver activates.

12. Click Screen Saver **D**elay and specify the *delay time* by entering a number or clicking the up or down arrow to increase or decrease the number.

13. Click OK to save the settings.

If you have problems...

If your screen saver appears too frequently while you are working, increase the delay time number.

Note: *To disable the screen saver, type **0** as the **D**elay time or set the Screen Saver N**a**me to (None).*

Some screen savers have a password option that you can enable. When this option is enabled, you must correctly enter the password before the normal desktop is restored to the screen.

To set a password for the Marquee screen saver, follow these steps:

1. In the Desktop dialog box, verify that the Marquee screen saver is selected.

2. Click Set**u**p.

3. In the Setup dialog box, click **P**assword Protected in the Password Options section.

4. Click **S**et Password.

The Change
Password dialog
box appears.

5. If a password already exists, type it in the **O**ld Password text box. An asterisk (*) appears for each character you type.

6. Enter the new password in the **N**ew Password text box and then enter the password again in the **R**etype New Password text box. Both passwords must match, and each can be up to 20 characters, including spaces. Passwords are not case sensitive.

7. Click OK. If the passwords match, the screen saver's Setup dialog box reappears. If the passwords do not match, you are prompted to enter the passwords again.

After the screen saver activates, you must type the correct password to return to your screen; otherwise, an error dialog box appears. If you are switching to a new screen saver and your old screen saver had a password, you must enter the old screen saver's password before you can enter a new password. Make sure that you don't forget the password!

Follow these steps to disable password checking:

1. Double-click the Desktop icon in Control Panel.

2. Click Set**u**p in the Screen Saver section.

3. Click **P**assword Protected in the Password Options section to deselect the check box.

4. Click OK.

Task: Enable Fast Switching

When you're running several programs at the same time—called *multitasking*—you want to be able to switch among them as quickly as possible. The Desktop dialog box enables you to turn on a "fast switching" option. With this option turned on, you can hold down the Alt key and repeatedly press the Tab key to cycle through currently running programs. While you're holding down the Alt key, Windows displays only the program names—not entire screens—which is how it saves time. When you release the Alt key, the program screen appears. (You can still press Alt+Tab to switch between running programs with the fast-switching option turned off, but it's slower.)

To turn on fast switching, follow these steps:

1. Double-click the Desktop icon in Control Panel.

2. Click Fast "A**l**t+Tab" Switching in the Applications section.

3. Click OK.

Task: Set the Date and Time

Date/Time

The Date/Time program will change the date or time currently set in your computer. For example, you may need to use this tool when daylight savings time comes or goes.

Follow these steps to adjust the date and time on your system:

1. Double-click the Date/Time icon in Control Panel.

Many programs use the Date/Time information when they automatically add the date or time to a file.

2. Double-click the month, date, or year value that you want to change in the **D**ate box. Either type the correct date or click one of the scroll arrows to scroll rapidly to the date you want.

3. Double-click the hour, minute, or second value that you want to change in the **T**ime box. Either type the correct time or click one of the scroll arrows to scroll rapidly to the time you want.

4. Click OK to save the changes to the date and time.

Note: *You can change the* format *for the date and time by using the International program.*

Fine-Tuning the Mouse

Mouse

The Mouse program is used to adjust the settings for your mouse. If you aren't comfortable with the way the mouse responds, you can adjust the sensitivity and speed. You can also reverse the left and right mouse button actions if you are left-handed.

Note: *Your mouse icon may look different, may appear as Mouse/Trackball if you have a trackball, or may offer different options or settings from those described in this section.*

Task: Change the Mouse Sensitivity

The **M**ouse Tracking Speed option controls how quickly the mouse will move across the screen. For example, if you have trouble selecting small portions of text, you may want to reduce the tracking speed to slow down the mouse.

Follow these steps to adjust the mouse sensitivity:

1. Double-click the Mouse icon in Control Panel.

The Mouse dialog box appears.

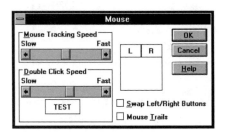

2. Click the left or right arrow on the **M**ouse Tracking Speed scroll bar to change the pointer's speed. Move left for a slower mouse or move right for a faster mouse.

3. Click OK to save your changes.

Task: Adjust the Double-Click Speed

If you find yourself double-clicking a program icon several times to get the program to run, you may need to adjust the double-click speed. Also, as you become a more proficient mouse user, you may want to speed up the response rate.

Follow these steps to adjust the double-click response:

1. In the Mouse dialog box, click the left or right arrow on the **D**ouble Click Speed scroll bar to decrease or increase the speed.

2. Double-click the TEST box to test the new rate (the colors reverse when you double-click successfully).

3. Click OK to save the changes.

Note: *Click **M**ouse Trails to leave a trail of arrows when you move the mouse. This feature is handy for laptop displays, which can redraw the screen too slowly to track a moving mouse pointer.*

Task: Swap the Mouse Buttons

If you are left-handed, you may want to switch the mouse button operation. Follow these steps to swap the mouse buttons:

1. In the Mouse dialog box, click **S**wap Left/Right Buttons.

The L and R in the test box change places when you select the **S**wap Left/Right Buttons option.

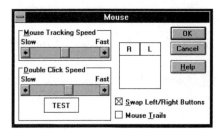

2. Place the mouse pointer inside the test box and click the left and right mouse buttons to highlight the L and R boxes. In this way, you can test the mouse buttons.

If you have problems...

If you swap the left and right buttons, you must click the right mouse button instead of the left mouse button for most purposes. For example, you must press the right mouse button to deselect the **S**wap Left/Right Buttons option.

Using Windows System Sounds

Use the Sound program to enable or disable system sounds. If you have a sound board installed (or a software-driven equivalent), you can use the Sound program to assign sounds to various computer events, such as a critical stop. If you do not have a sound board, the default sound for all events is a beep.

Note: *You can use the Windows speaker driver to play many system sounds. To obtain the speaker driver (SPEAKER.DRV), contact Microsoft or see Que's book* Killer Windows Utilities.

Task: Turn Sounds Off

If you are tired of listening to your computer announce your mistakes with a beep, or when you need to hide the fact that you're playing a game, you can turn off the computer's sound.

Follow these steps to turn off system sounds:

1. Double-click the Sound icon in Control Panel.

The Sound dialog
box appears.

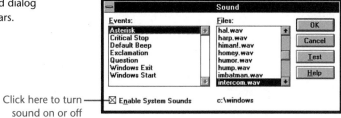

Click here to turn
sound on or off

2. Deselect the E**n**able System Sounds check box.

3. Click OK.

This action disables all sounds for all programs used in Windows.

Task: Assign a Sound to an Event

If your computer is equipped with a sound board (as are all multimedia
PCs), you can assign sounds to various computer events, such as exiting
Windows. Certain software programs can give you sound capabilities
even if you don't have a sound board. If you don't have a sound board,
the Windows speaker driver (described in an earlier note in "Using Windows System Sounds"), or the appropriate software, the **F**iles and **E**vents
options will be grayed.

Sounds are stored in waveform files, with a WAV extension. Windows
comes with four predefined sounds, and you can purchase additional
WAV files.

To assign sounds to events, follow these steps:

1. Double-click the Sound icon in Control Panel.

2. In the **E**vents list, click the event to which you want to assign
sound.

3. In the **F**iles list, click the sound to be assigned to the event you
selected.

4. Click **T**est to hear a sample of your sound.

5. Click OK.

Summary

To	Do This
Open the Control Panel group window	Double-click the Main group icon. Double-click the Control Panel group icon.
Change the screen colors	Double-click the Colors icon in Control Panel. Select a color scheme from the Color **S**chemes drop-down list. Click OK.
Customize a color scheme	Double-click the Colors icon in Control Panel. Select a color scheme from the Color **S**chemes drop-down list. Click Color **P**alette. Click the element whose color you want to change. Click the color in the **B**asic Colors palette. To save your changes, click S**a**ve Scheme and then type a name in the text box in the Save Scheme dialog box. Or click Cancel to cancel your changes.
Select a desktop pattern	Double-click the Desktop icon in Control Panel. Select a pattern from the Pattern **N**ame drop-down list. Click OK.
Select a wallpaper	Double-click the Desktop icon in Control Panel. Select a wallpaper file from the Wallpaper **F**ile drop-down list. Click **T**ile or **C**enter. Click OK.
Turn on the screen saver	Double-click the Desktop icon in Control Panel. Select a design from the Screen Saver N**a**me drop-down list. Specify the delay time. Click OK.
Set a password with the screen saver	Double-click the Desktop icon in Control Panel. If necessary, select a screen saver and specify the delay time. Click Set**u**p, **P**assword Protected, and then **S**et Password. Type the old password, if necessary. Type the new password and then retype it. Click OK.
Disable password checking	Double-click the Desktop icon in Control Panel. Click Set**u**p. Click Password **P**rotected to remove the X in the check box, thus disabling the password.
Enable fast switching between programs	Double-click the Desktop icon in Control Panel. Click Fast "A**l**t+Tab" Switching in the Applications section. Click OK.
Set the date and time	Double-click the Date/Time icon in Control Panel. Click **D**ate or **T**ime. Press Tab to cycle through the values; type the correct date or time, or click the up or down arrow to increase or decrease the value. Click OK.

To	Do This
Adjust the mouse sensitivity	Double-click the Mouse icon in Control Panel. Click the left or right arrow on the **M**ouse Tracking Speed scroll bar for a slower or faster mouse response. Click OK.
Adjust the double-click speed	Double-click the Mouse icon in Control Panel. Click the left or right arrow on the **D**ouble Click Speed scroll bar to decrease or increase the double-click speed. Double-click the TEST box to test the new rate. Click OK.
Swap the mouse buttons	Double-click the Mouse icon in Control Panel. Click **S**wap Left/Right Buttons. Click OK.
Turn sounds on or off	Double-click the Sound icon in Control Panel. Select or deselect the E**n**able System Sounds check box. Click OK.
Assign a sound to an event	Double-click the Sound icon in Control Panel. Click the event in the **E**vents list. Click the sound in the **F**iles list. Click **T**est to hear the selected sound. Click OK.

On Your Own
Estimated time: 15 minutes

1. Look at the rest of the predefined Windows color schemes.

2. Select the Honey wallpaper and tile it across the desktop.

3. Select the Winlogo wallpaper and center it on the Spinner desktop pattern.

4. Set up the Marquee screen saver with your company name in large, italicized, dark-blue text on a light gray background. Specify a delay time of five minutes.

5. Check the accuracy of your system clock and make any necessary adjustments.

6. Turn on mouse trails.

7. If you have a sound board, assign several sound files to system events.

Controlling Printers and Fonts

Windows programs share more than a common graphical interface. They share printing resources also. Windows' Print Manager manages printing for all Windows programs, transferring information and instructions to your printer while you continue working.

Windows 3.11 includes a selection of TrueType fonts, which you can use in all Windows programs. You can purchase additional TrueType fonts and install them easily through the Fonts program in Control Panel.

This lesson shows you how to

- Select a default printer
- Share a printer
- Pause and resume a print job
- Manage print jobs
- Connect to a network printer
- Disconnect from a network printer
- Turn Print Manager on and off
- Install a new printer
- Configure a printer
- View TrueType fonts
- Turn True Type fonts off
- Install additional fonts

Local Printing versus Network Printing

During Windows installation, you have the option to install one or more printers. You must have at least one printer installed in order to print in Windows. If you skipped the step in the installation or if you gain access to another printer, you can install additional printers with the Printers program.

Both *local printers* (those directly connected to your computer) and *network printers* (those connected to a local area network) can be managed with Print Manager. Additional options are available in Print Manager if you print to a network printer, such as viewing the print queue for the entire network and updating the network print queue status. You can also bypass Print Manager altogether, which can speed up printing on a network.

Using Print Manager

Print queue
A list of print jobs waiting to be printed.

When you print a document in a Windows program, Print Manager takes over. First, Windows sends the file to Print Manager, where files are lined up in a *print queue*, waiting to be printed. Print Manager then routes the files, in the order received, to your printer. This approach differs from that of most DOS programs in which you have to wait for the print job to finish before you can continue working. With Print Manager taking over, you can continue working and even exit that application and start working in another one, as long as you don't exit Windows.

Print Manager works only with programs designed for Windows. DOS programs running in Windows don't use Print Manager. A DOS program prints just as though it weren't in Windows. DOS programs cannot share the common printer drivers used by Windows programs. Therefore, you must complete the printer installation and setup required for each DOS program.

The Print Manager window shows the status of your print queue. You can see which printer or printers are active, which printer is printing, which file is being printed, what other files are queued for printing, and optionally the file's size and the time and date you sent the file to the printer.

The default printer is underlined; to change a print queue, just click the icon for the printer you want to change.

Shared printer icon

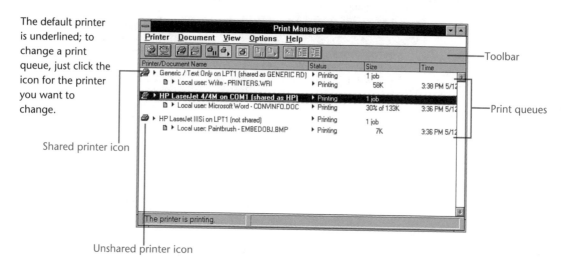

Toolbar

Print queues

Unshared printer icon

WfW   Windows 3.11 for Workgroups installs a toolbar in Print Manager to make it easier to execute common menu commands. Table 6.1 lists all the buttons available if your Windows for Workgroups is installed with network capabilities. If your system has Windows 3.11 for Workgroups with the network capability turned off, you may not see all these buttons on your toolbar.

Table 6.1 Print Manager Toolbar Buttons

Button Name	Button	Description
Connect Network Printer		Connects to a shared printer
Disconnect Network Printer		Disconnects from a shared printer
Share Printer As		Shares your printer with other people; adds or changes a comment or password
Stop Sharing Printer		Stops sharing your printer with other people
Pause Printer		Temporarily stops your printer from printing
Resume Printer		Restarts a paused printer

6

(continues)

Table 6.1 Continued

Button Name	Button	Description
Set Default Printer		Specifies the selected printer as the default printer
Pause Printing Document		Suspends printing a document
Resume Printing Document		Resumes printing a paused document
Delete Document		Deletes a print job from your print queue or a network print queue
Move Document Up		Moves a print job up in the queue, making it print sooner
Move Document Down		Moves a print job down in the queue, making it print later

Task: Select a Default Printer

Default printer
The printer you use most often; print jobs are sent to this printer automatically unless you change the setup.

If you have only one printer installed in Windows, it is automatically defined as the *default printer*. If you have access to more than one printer (local or network), you must designate one of those printers as the default. You can easily change this designation if that printer is unavailable. In addition, most Windows programs have a Print Setup dialog box where you can select a different printer before the print job is sent.

Follow these steps to select the default printer:

1. Double-click the Print Manager icon in the Main group window.

2. Select the printer from the Printer/Document Name list.

3. Pull down the **P**rinter menu and choose Set **D**efault Printer.

   or

   Click the Set Default Printer button on the toolbar.

Sharing Your Printer

WfW

If you are using Windows 3.11 for Workgroups, you can share your printer with other people on a network. Sharing may be useful if the network printer is "down" and your printer is the closest alternative.

Depending on how long you want to share your printer, you can specify whether to share the printer automatically when you start Windows. You can add a comment to be displayed next to the name of the printer in the Connect Network Printer dialog box; this comment might indicate, for example, how long the printer will be available or whether the printer requires special paper.

Note: *If you chose Yes in the Do You Want to Share Printer Now dialog box when you installed Windows 3.11 for Workgroups, your printer is already shared.*

Follow these steps to designate a printer as shared:

1. Open Print Manager.

2. From the Print Manager window, select the printer you want to share.

3. Pull down the **Printer** menu and choose **Share** Printer As.

   or

   Click the Share Printer As button on the toolbar.

Specify the Shared Printer name and add a comment and password, if necessary, in the Share Printer dialog box.

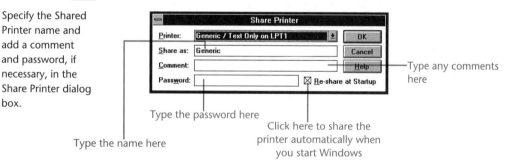

Type any comments here

Type the password here

Click here to share the printer automatically when you start Windows

Type the name here

6

The name you specify in the **Share** As text box will be used by other people on your network to select your printer. Try to choose a name that indicates clearly which printer is which, especially if your network includes a number of local printers. The Comment information may include details about the printer—for example, that it requires a special type of print ribbon, toner, or paper. Adding a password ensures that only those users who know the password can access the printer.

To stop sharing a printer, follow these steps:

1. Open Print Manager.

2. Pull down the **Printer** menu and choose **St**op Sharing Printer.

   or

    Click the Stop Sharing Printer button on the toolbar.

Use the Stop Sharing Printer dialog box to select one or more printers to stop sharing with others.

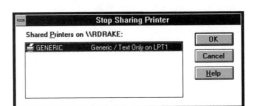

3. From the Shared **P**rinters list, select the printer.

4. Click OK.

   Note: *You can extend the selection to include more than one printer.*

Managing Print Jobs

Print Manager has options that enable you to pause and resume the printing of a certain document or the use of a certain printer. For example, you might pause a long document to print a rush job in the middle, or pause a printer to change toner or load paper. On your own printer, you can pause anyone else's document as long as it hasn't started printing yet. You cannot pause your own documents. On a network printer you are connected to, you can pause only your own documents if they are not already printing. You can pause your printer, but not a network printer.

Task: Pause and Resume a Document Print Job

Follow these steps to pause the printing of a document:

1. Open Print Manager.

2. Select the document in the Print Manager window.

3. Pull down the **Document** menu and choose **Pa**use Printing Document.

or

 Click the Pause Printing Document button on the toolbar.

The status of the selected document changes to indicate that printing has been paused.

Follow these steps to resume the printing of a paused document:

1. Double-click the Print Manager icon in the Main group window.

2. Select the paused document in the Print Manager window.

3. Pull down the Document menu and choose Resume Printing Document.

   or

 Click the Resume Printing Document button on the toolbar.

Task: Pause and Resume a Print Queue

Follow these steps to pause a printer:

1. Open Print Manager.

2. Select the printer in the Print Manager window.

3. Pull down the Printer menu and choose Pause Printer.

   or

Click the Pause Printer button on the toolbar.

6

Pausing the printer doesn't stop the print job; the printer just waits for you to resume the print queue.

Click here to resume a paused printer

Click here to pause the printer

Selected printer

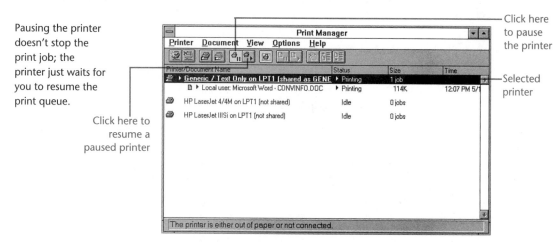

The status of the selected printer changes to indicate that printing has been paused.

Follow these steps to resume a paused printer:

1. Double-click the Print Manager icon in the Main group window.

2. Select the paused printer in the Print Manager window.

3. Pull down the **Pr**inter menu and choose **Resume Printer.**

or

Click the Resume Printer button on the toolbar.

Task: Change the Order of Print Jobs in the Queue

You can rearrange the order of print jobs (as long as they haven't started printing yet) on your local printer, whether it is shared or not. If you are printing to a network printer, you can change the order of only your own documents, and you can move them downward only.

Follow these steps to rearrange the print order:

1. Open Print Manager.

2. Select the document in the Print Manager window.

3. Pull down the **D**ocument menu and choose Move Document Up or Move Document Down.

or

Click the Move Document Up or Move Document Down button on the toolbar.

or

Click and drag the document to a new position.

Task: Cancel a Print Job

If you need to cancel a print job, you delete the document from the queue. In a network print queue, you can delete only your own documents and only if they haven't started printing. To cancel all print jobs on your printer (shared or not shared), exit the Print Manager.

Follow these steps to cancel the printing of a document:

1. Double-click the Print Manager icon in the Main group window.

2. Select the document in the Print Manager window.

3. Pull down the Document menu and choose Delete Document.

or

Click the Delete Document button on the toolbar.

Print Manager asks you to confirm the deletion of a print job.

4. Click OK in the Print Manager message box to confirm the cancellation.

Task: Connect to a Network Printer

If a network is installed in Windows 3.11 for Workgroups on your computer, you can print on a network printer. First, though, you must be sure that you are connected through the network to the printer you want to use. You can do this while you are installing a printer or when using the Print Manager window.

To connect to a network printer, follow these steps:

1. Double-click the Print Manager icon in the Main group window.

2. Pull down the Printer menu and choose Connect Network Printer.

or

Click the Connect Network Printer button on the toolbar.

6

You specify the path and port or a network for the network printer in the Connect Network Printer dialog box.

3. In the **Path** text box, type the path for the printer. Select the port you want to use; then click OK.

or

Click the button for your network. For example, if you are using NetWare, click NetWare.

You specify the port and path for your network printer in the Network-Printer Connections dialog box.

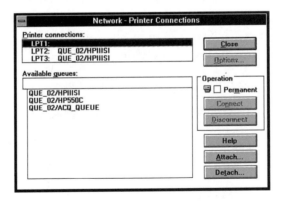

4. Select the port and path of the printer to which you want to connect. Click Connect and then Close.

| **If you have problems...** | If you don't see the network printer listed, it hasn't been configured in Windows yet. Consult your network administrator. |

The Print Manager will display a print queue for network printers and for local printers. You can see all the files that are queued up to a network printer, even if they are not your print jobs. This list gives you an idea of how long it will be before the printer gets to your job.

Task: Disconnect from a Network Printer

If you are finished using a network printer, you can disconnect from it. You will have to disconnect the printer if you want to connect a different network printer to the same port.

To disconnect from a network printer, follow these steps:

1. Open Print Manager.

2. Pull down the **P**rinter menu and choose Disconnect Network Printer.

    or

    Click the Disconnect Network Printer button on the toolbar.

3. Select the printer you want to disconnect.

    Note: *You can extend the selection to more than one printer, enabling you to disconnect multiple printers at once.*

4. Click OK.

Task: Turn Print Manager Off

In most cases, printing is faster when you bypass the Print Manager queue and print files directly to the network queue. Printing directly to the network queue, therefore, is the Print Manager's default choice. Because networks differ, however, experiment with printing times on your own network to find out whether printing directly to a network printer is faster than using Print Manager.

6

To print directly to a network printer, follow these steps:

1. Open Print Manager.

2. Pull down the **Options** menu and choose **Background Printing**.

3. Select the **Send** Documents Directly to Network check box so that an X appears in it.

   Note: *When you send a print job directly to a network printer or a network print spooler, no Print Manager icon appears at the bottom of the Windows desktop.*

4. Click OK.

Task: Install a New Printer

Printer driver
Tells Windows how to control your printer and use its features.

You can easily add printers that were not initially installed with Windows. To do this, you probably will need your original Windows installation disks or the disk from your printer's manufacturer that contains the Windows *printer driver* for your printer.

To install a new printer, follow these steps:

1. Open Print Manager.

2. Pull down the **Options** menu and choose **Printer Setup**.

The Printers dialog box appears.

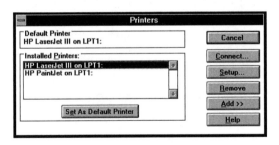

3. Click the Add button.

Note: *You can also open the Printers dialog box by double-clicking the Printers icon in Control Panel.*

The bottom of the
Printers dialog box
expands to display
a list of printers.

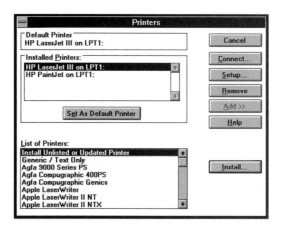

The printers in the List of Printers list box are those that came with
your Windows installation disks. All Windows programs use these
printers.

4. From the List of Printers list box, select the printer you want to
install.

If your printer's model is not listed, select an earlier model from the
manufacturer's same family of printers. If you have a disk from
your printer's manufacturer that contains the Windows driver for
your printer, select Install Unlisted or Updated Printer (appearing
out of alphabetic order at the top of the list).

5. Click the Install button.

If you are installing a new driver you have not used before or you
are updating an existing driver, Windows displays the Install Driver
dialog box, prompting you to insert in drive A the disk containing
the printer driver.

A message at the
top of the box
specifies which disk
to insert.

6

6. Insert the requested disk.

7. If necessary, change the path to another drive or directory where the files are located.

Windows adds the printer driver to the Installed Printers list and connects the driver to the LPT1 port.

If you have problems...

If you don't have a printer driver for your printer, call Microsoft or the printer's manufacturer to see whether one has been written, or use a printer driver for an earlier model of the same printer. Another alternative is to select the Generic/Text Only printer from the List of Printers list box. This selection enables most printers to print but doesn't use any enhanced features, such as graphics, fonts, styles, or sizes.

Task: Configure a Printer

After you add your printer to the Installed Printers list, you need to connect the printer to a printer port. (By default, Windows connects all new printers to LPT1; if this port is the right one, you can bypass this procedure.) After you tell Windows which port the printer is connected to, you can set up the printer for special features, such as font cartridges, paper size, bins, and printing orientation.

To configure the printer for a port, follow these steps:

1. Open Print Manager.

2. Pull down the Options menu and choose Printer Setup.

3. Select the printer from the Installed Printers list.

4. Click the Connect button.

The Connect dialog box appears.

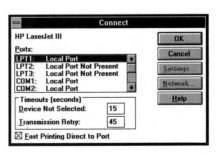

5. From the **P**orts list box, select the hardware port (the connection for the printer cable) to which the printer you selected is connected. (Most printers are connected to LPT1. If you are not sure, experiment with other ports or call your dealer or PC administrator.)

   Note: *If you have a parallel printer connected to LPT1 or LPT2, but the printer does not work when you select either port from the Ports list, select instead LPT1.DOS or LPT2.DOS from the Ports list.*

6. Select timeout settings as defined by your printer manual or the README.TXT file for your printer. (Read the file with Notepad.) If no information is available for your printer, leave these settings as they are.

7. Click OK to save the Connect settings.

8. In the Printers dialog box, click the **S**etup button to display your printer's printer setup dialog box.

   Note: *To change the printer setup at a later time while you are in a Windows program, you can use the program's **File Print Setup** command.*

Because each printer has different capabilities, each printer setup dialog box may be different. This example shows the printer setup dialog box for the HP LaserJet III printer family.

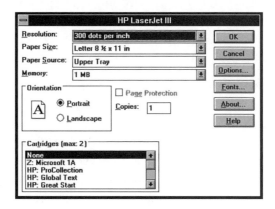

6

Typically, the printer setup dialog box asks you to specify the paper size and source, the number of copies you want to print, and the page orientation (*portrait* for vertical printing or *landscape* for horizontal printing). Depending on the printer, you have other options as well. For example, you must select the font cartridges you plan to use with your HP LaserJet III printer.

> **Note:** *If your printer accepts two font cartridges, you can select both cartridges from the Cartridges list: click one cartridge, scroll to the second one, and click the second cartridge.*

9. Select the printer options you use most frequently.

10. Click OK to return to the Printers dialog box.

11. Click OK to return to Print Manager.

Working with TrueType Fonts

Gone are the days of limited font selections—when the one or two fonts that came with your printer were all you had. Fortunately, the days of complex solutions to the problem of limited font selections are gone also. TrueType brings you easily accessible, built-in, scalable fonts that you can use with any kind of printer or computer. Although Windows comes equipped with only a few TrueType fonts, you can easily add more fonts to your system.

You aren't limited to using only TrueType fonts with Windows, however. If you have already invested in downloadable fonts, you can still use them. However, the manner in which a Windows application selects fonts may make it impossible to use some of those fonts.

TrueType fonts have several advantages over downloadable or printer-resident fonts. First, TrueType fonts include matching screen and printer fonts so that the appearance on-screen matches the printed copy. Second, TrueType fonts are used with virtually all Windows programs. If two computers have the same TrueType fonts installed, you can create a document on the first computer and print it on the second computer without losing the original appearance. TrueType fonts print on all types of printers, although the appearance varies with the quality of the printer.

Task: View Installed Fonts

The Fonts program in Control Panel manages the TrueType fonts in Windows. The Fonts dialog box lists the currently installed fonts. Commands in the Fonts dialog box enable you to add and remove fonts and set TrueType options.

Follow these steps to view the installed TrueType fonts:

1. Double-click the Fonts icon in Control Panel.

2. Use the scroll bar to scroll through the list.

3. Select a font in the list to view the sample text.

The Sample box shows you what the selected font looks like.

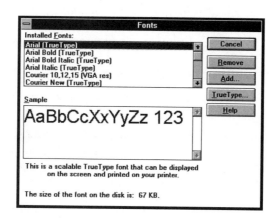

Task: Turn TrueType Fonts Off

By default, TrueType is turned on in Windows, but TrueType fonts consume memory on your computer and may be slower to display than other fonts. If your computer has limited memory or runs slowly, you may want to turn TrueType fonts off.

Follow these steps to turn TrueType fonts off:

1. Double-click the Fonts icon in Control Panel.

2. Click the TrueType button.

In the TrueType dialog box, you can turn TrueType Fonts on and off or choose to display only TrueType fonts in Windows applications.

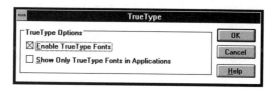

3. To turn TrueType fonts off, deselect the Enable TrueType Fonts option so that no X appears in the check box.

4. To display only TrueType fonts in your programs, select the **Show Only TrueType Fonts in Applications** option. (This option is not available if you have deselected the **Enable TrueType Fonts** option.)

5. Click OK.

   If you turn TrueType fonts off, a dialog box advises that you must restart Windows for your change to take effect.

6. To restart Windows, click the **Restart Now** button.

Task: Install New Fonts

You can easily add new fonts to your system, whether they are TrueType fonts or another type of font. To install TrueType fonts, use the Fonts program in Control Panel. Other types of fonts, such as Adobe Type Manager, come with their own installation procedures.

To add new TrueType fonts, follow these steps:

1. Double-click the Fonts icon in Control Panel.

2. Click the Add button.

You select font directories from the **D**irectories list box to add those fonts to the List of **F**onts in the Add Fonts dialog box.

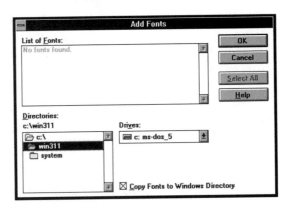

3. From the Drives list, select the drive containing the font you want to add.

4. From the Directories list, select the directory containing the font you want to add.

The fonts in the directory and drive you selected appear in the List of Fonts box.

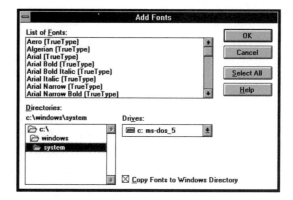

5. From the List of Fonts box, select the font or fonts you want to add.

or

If you want to add all the fonts, click the Select All button.

6. If you don't want to add the fonts to your system, but instead want to use them from the drive and directory where they're currently located, deselect the Copy Fonts to Windows Directory check box so that no X appears there.

7. Click OK to add the font or fonts to your system.

8. Click Close to close the Fonts dialog box.

If you are installing a new font cartridge, you must define that in the Printer program. See the section "Task: Configure a Printer" earlier in this lesson. If you are installing another type of font, consult the font program installation instructions.

Summary

To	Do This
Select a default printer	Double-click the Print Manager icon in the Main group window. Select the desired printer from the Printer/Document Name list. Pull down the Printer menu and choose Set Default Printer, or click the Set Default Printer button on the toolbar.

(continues)

To	Do This
Share a printer	Double-click the Print Manager icon in the Main group window. Select the printer you want to share. Pull down the **P**rinter menu and choose **S**hare Printer As, or click the Share Printer As button on the toolbar.
Stop sharing a printer	Double-click the Print Manager icon in the Main group window. Pull down the **P**rinter menu and choose Stop Sharing Printer, or click the Stop Sharing Printer button on the toolbar. Select the printer you want to stop sharing.
Pause printing a document	Double-click the Print Manager icon in the Main group window. Select the document in the Print Manager window. Pull down the **D**ocument menu and choose **P**ause Printing Document, or click the Pause Printing Document button on the toolbar.
Resume printing a document	Double-click the Print Manager icon in the Main group window. Select the document in the Print Manager window. Pull down the **D**ocument menu and choose **R**esume Printing Document, or click the Resume Printing Document button on the toolbar.
Resume a printer	Double-click the Print Manager icon in the Main group window. Select the printer in the Print Manager window. Pull down the **P**rinter menu and choose **R**esume Printer, or click the Resume Printer button on the toolbar.
Pause a printer	Double-click the Print Manager icon in the Main group window. Select the printer in the Print Manager window. Pull down the **P**rinter menu and choose **P**ause Printer, or click the Pause Printer button on the toolbar.
Rearrange the print order	Double-click the Print Manager icon in the Main group window. Select the document in the Print Manager window. Pull down the **D**ocument menu and choose Move Document **U**p or Move Document Down, or click the Move Document Up or Move Document Down button on the toolbar.
Cancel printing a document	Double-click the Print Manager icon in the Main group window. Select the document in the Print Manager window. Pull down the **D**ocument menu and choose **D**elete Document, or click the Delete Document button on the toolbar. Click OK to confirm the cancellation.
Connect to a Network Printer	Double-click the Print Manager icon in the Maingroup window. Pull down the **P**rinter menu and choose Connect Network Printer, or click the connect Network Printer button on the toolbar. Type the path for the printer in the

To	Do This
	Path text box. Select the port you want to use; then click OK. Or click the button for your network (for example, NetWare). Select the port and path of the printer to which you want to connect. Click Connect and then Close.
Disconnect from a network	Double-click the Print Manager icon in the Main group window Pull down the Printer menu and choose Disconnect Network Printer, or click the Disconnect Network Printer button on the toolbar. Select the printer you want to disconnect. Click OK.
Turn Print Manager off for network printers	Double-click the Print Manager icon in the Main group window. Pull down the Options menu and choose Background Printing. Select the Send Documents Directly to Network check box so that an X appears in it. Click OK.
Install a new printer	Double-click the Print Manager icon in the Main group window. Pull down the Options menu and choose Printer Setup. Click the Add button. From the list, select the printer you want to install. Click the Install button. Insert the required disk. If necessary, change the path to the drive or directory where the files are located.
Configure a printer	Double-click the Print Manager icon in the Main group window. Pull down the Options menu and choose Printer Setup. From the Installed Printers list, select the printer you want to configure. Click the Connect button. Select a port from the Ports list. If necessary, change the timeout settings. Click OK to save the changes. Click the Setup button to open the printer setup dialog box. Select the printer options you use most frequently. Click OK twice.
View installed fonts	Double-click the Fonts icon in Control Panel. Use the scroll bar to scroll through the list. Select a font to see the sample text.
Turn TrueType fonts off	Double-click the Fonts icon in Control Panel. Click the TrueType button. Deselect the Enable TrueType Fonts option so that no X appears in the check box. Click OK.
Install new fonts	Double-click the Fonts icon in Control Panel. Click the Add button. From the Drives list, select the drive containing the font you want to add. From the Directories list, select the directory containing the font you want to add. From the List of Fonts box, select the font(s) you want to add. Click OK.

6

On Your Own
Estimated time: 15 minutes

1. Select your own default printer.

2. If you are on a network, set up a printer to share with your coworkers. Then go through the steps to stop sharing the printer.

3. If you are on a network, connect to a network printer (different from the one shared in the preceding step).

4. Disconnect from the network printer you connected to in the preceding step.

5. If you need to, install and configure a new printer.

6. View all the TrueType fonts in your list of fonts.

7. If you have them available, install additional TrueType fonts on your system.

Part III
Managing Files with File Manager

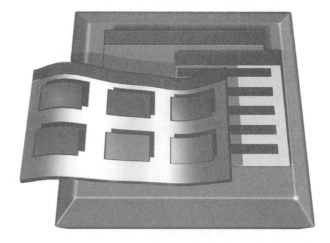

Displaying and Organizing Files

File Manager in Windows is a well-designed tool that acts like an office manager. It displays information about the files and directories on your drives and helps you locate specific files.

In this lesson, you learn how to

- Develop a directory structure
- Identify parts of the File Manager window
- View the contents of a directory
- Identify different types of file icons
- Display file size, last modification date, last modification time, and file attributes
- Expand and collapse directories
- Display file and directory information for a different drive on your system
- Open and arrange multiple directory windows
- Search for files
- Sort a file list
- Use the File Manager toolbar
- Create a file association
- Start a program from File Manager

Task: Develop a Directory Structure

Directory

An area on a hard disk where files and programs can be grouped together by type or category. A directory is similar to a drawer in a file cabinet.

Subdirectory

A directory within a directory. A subdirectory is similar to a folder within a file drawer.

To make the job of finding files easier, hard disks are usually organized into *directories*. If you think of your hard disk as a filing cabinet, directories are like the drawers in the filing cabinet. In a filing cabinet, each drawer can hold a different collection of documents. In a hard disk, each directory can hold a different category of files. The files in a directory can be programs or documents.

Within a filing cabinet drawer, you can put hanging folders to segment the drawer further. Within a hard disk, you can segment a directory by putting *subdirectories* below it. These subdirectories can also contain files. For example, you may want a DOCS directory for word processing jobs, and within the DOCS directory, you may want subdirectories with names such as BUDGETS, PROPOSAL, LETTERS, and REPORTS.

You can continue to segment a subdirectory by creating subdirectories below it. For example, under the REPORTS subdirectory, you might create subdirectories called ANNUAL, QTRLY, STATUS, and MISC. The subdirectories of a subdirectory can be compared to the manila folders within a hanging folder.

Consider some other examples of directory structures: FINANCES, CORRES, GAMES, and HOMEWORK; JEFF, BEN, and LAURA; HOMES, APTS, DUPLEXES, and CONDOS; and BOOKS, ARTICLES, and JOURNALS.

The type of directory structure you choose for your system is determined by the type of files you work with. You may want to start by examining your paper filing system for ideas on how your documents can be organized on your hard disk. Keep in mind that you can make changes to your directory structure as it becomes necessary, so it isn't "written in stone."

Directory tree
A diagram showing how directories and subdirectories are related.

File Manager displays directories and subdirectories in a *directory tree* format. A directory tree is similar to a family tree. The root directory is at the top, and a directory that contains subdirectories is described as the *parent* directory. File Manager displays a directory tree with the drive letter at the top (root), directories listed in alphabetic order, and subdirectories that appear below and slightly to the right of their parent directories.

Task: Start File Manager

The File Manager program icon is located in the Main group window. If you use File Manager often, you may want to copy the program icon into your other group windows. See Lesson 3, "Working with Groups and Applications," for more information about moving and copying program icons between groups.

The File Manager icon looks like a file cabinet.

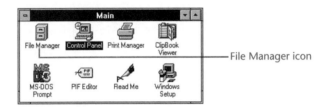

File Manager icon

Exploring the File Manager Window

Contents list
A displayed list of files and directories for the selected drive or directory.

When you first start File Manager, a directory window of the Windows directory is displayed. The directory window is divided into two parts. The directory tree, with the expanded structure of directories and subdirectories on the Windows drive, occupies the left portion of the window. The *contents list* occupies the right portion of the window, showing the files (and subdirectories) in the selected directory. The title bar for the window shows the directory path for the selected directory.

7

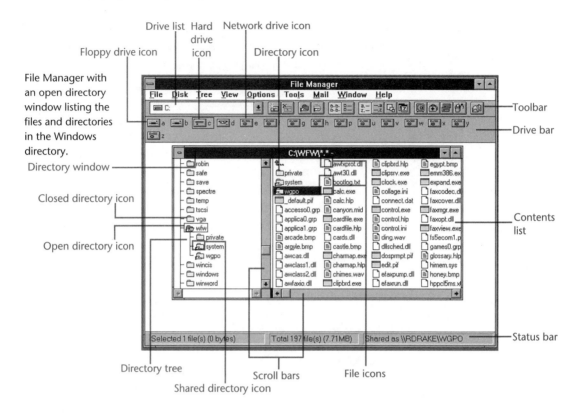

Floppy drive icon · Drive list · Hard drive icon · Network drive icon · Directory icon · File Manager with an open directory window listing the files and directories in the Windows directory. · Directory window · Closed directory icon · Open directory icon · Toolbar · Drive bar · Contents list · Status bar · Directory tree · Shared directory icon · Scroll bars · File icons

WfW — Windows 3.11 for Workgroups installs a toolbar in the File Manager window, much like the toolbar in the File Manager window for Windows 3.11. If you have only Windows 3.11 installed on your system, you will not see a toolbar here (or in Print Manager).

Note: *When you first start File Manager, the directory window is not maximized. Maximize the window to see more files and directories.*

The directory tree uses miniature folders as icons to indicate directories and subdirectories. An open folder icon indicates that the directory's contents are shown in the contents list.

Selection cursor

A dotted rectangular bar used to select drives, directories, or files in the File Manager directory window.

At any given time, only one area of File Manager is active: the drive bar, the directory tree, or the contents list. The active area contains a rectangular area of the same color as the title bar. This area is called the *selection cursor*. You can select an area with the mouse by clicking on it.

Note: *You can also press the Tab key to cycle through the drive bar, the directory tree, and the contents list.*

The right side of the status bar always displays the number and aggregate size of the files in the selected directory or subdirectory. When the directory tree portion of the window is active, the left portion of the bar shows the drive letter, total size, and free space on the selected drive. When the contents list is active, this area shows the size and the date and time of the selected file; if multiple files are selected, this area shows the total number and size of the selected files.

Task: View the Contents of a Directory

The directory window is always displayed in the File Manager window. It may be either in its own open window within the File Manager window, or as an icon at the bottom of the File Manager window. The directory tree (in the left half of the directory window) shows the hierarchical structure of the area of the drive you are currently examining.

In the sample directory window, drive C contains a WFW directory with three subdirectories: CLIPART, SCS, and WINWORD.CBT. The SCS subdirectory contains a subdirectory named INTRO.

File Manager uses lines to indicate the relationship between directories and subdirectories.

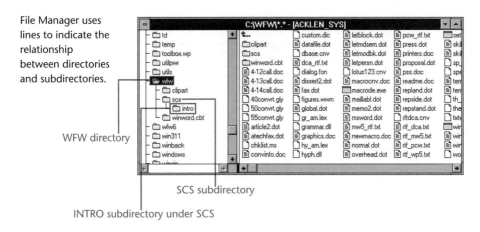

WFW directory

SCS subdirectory

INTRO subdirectory under SCS

7

You can select only one directory at a time in a given directory window; however, you can open multiple directories so that each appears in its own directory window. Open more than one directory when you want to see the contents of multiple directories at once. Copying files between directories is easier when you open a source directory window and a destination directory window. For more information, see "Task: Open Multiple Directory Windows" later in this lesson.

Follow these steps to select the directory or subdirectory you want:

1. Double-click the File Manager icon in the Main group window.

2. Select a directory name from the directory tree to display a list of that directory's files in the contents list.

If you have problems...   If you cannot see the directory you want, use the vertical scroll bar in the directory tree to scroll the directory into sight before selecting it. If you need to see files in a subdirectory, first open the directory above that subdirectory.

Understanding File and Directory Icons

The contents list uses four different types of file icons to indicate the type of a given file. Two directory icons are used to distinguish between a shared and nonshared directory. The shared directory icon will appear only if you are connected to a network. Table 7.1 illustrates the different icons and their descriptions.

Table 7.1 File and Directory Icons	
Icon	**Description**
📄	Document files associated with an application. When you select a document file, the application is started, and the file is opened.
▭	Program files, batch files, and PIF files. These files start applications.
🛈	Files with system or hidden attributes.
🗋	All other files.
🗁	Directories shared with other users on the network.
🗀	Directories not shared with other users on the network.

Task: Display File Information

You can specify what file information appears in the contents list by choosing options from the **V**iew menu. For the two most common displays, you use **V**iew **N**ame to show only the file names and extensions, or **V**iew **A**ll File Details to show all file information. A third option, **V**iew **P**artial Details, enables you to select which details you want to see. Finally, you can choose to view only certain types of files (programs, documents, and so on).

To modify the way your file information is displayed, follow these steps:

1. Double-click the File Manager icon in the Main group window.

2. Select the directory window you want to change.

3. Open the **V**iew menu and choose one of these options:

Command	Description
Name	Displays only names and directories.
All File Details	Displays the name, size, date and time last saved, and file attributes.
Partial Details	Displays a Partial Details dialog box where you can select from size, last modification date, last modification time, and file attributes.
By File **T**ype	Displays files by type: program, document, directory, and other. You can choose to view hidden and system files as well. You can also use DOS wild-card characters to view files by a portion of the file name.

In this example, the contents list displays only file names.

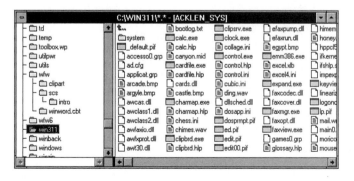

7

In this example, the contents list displays all file details: name, size, date and time the file was last saved, and file attributes.

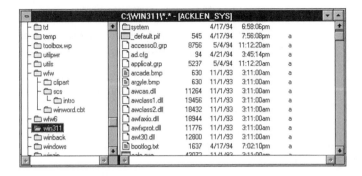

Note: *Some programs may not automatically update the information in File Manager. As a result, you may activate File Manager and not see a file you have just saved. You can update the window manually with* **W***indow* **R***efresh.*

Task: Expand and Collapse a Directory

Expand
To show additional directory levels below a selected directory.

Collapse
To hide additional directory levels below a selected directory.

After you select a specific directory, you may want to *expand* the directory so that you can see the subdirectories below it. Or you may want to *collapse* the fully expanded directory structure to see the directories at a higher level. Notice the lines and indentations that show how directories and subdirectories are dependent.

The directory icon for an expanded directory changes to an open manila folder. When the directory is collapsed, the directory icon changes back to a closed folder. These changes apply to both shared and nonshared directory icons.

Collapsed directories do not show the subdirectories they contain.

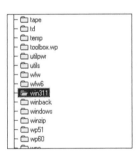

Expanded directories show all the subdirectories located below them.

To expand or collapse a directory or subdirectory without using menu commands, perform the following actions:

Action	Result
Double-click the collapsed directory name.	The directory expands.
Double-click the expanded directory name.	The directory collapses.

Note: *If you prefer, File Manager will display a plus sign (+) in the directory icon of each expandable directory, and a minus sign (–) in the directory icon of each collapsable directory. Pull down the **T**ree menu and choose **I**ndicate Expandable Branches.*

To expand or collapse directories by using menu commands, follow these steps:

1. Select the directory or subdirectory.

2. Pull down the **T**ree menu and choose one of the following commands:

Command	Description
E**x**pand One Level	Expands the selected directory to show all subdirectories at the next lower level
Expand **B**ranch	Expands the selected directory to show all lower subdirectories at any level
Expand **A**ll	Expands all subdirectories in the drive
Collapse Branch	Collapses all lower-level subdirectories in the selected directory

7

Task: Change to a Different Drive

Sometimes the files you need to work with are on a different drive, such as a floppy drive or network drive. Several methods for displaying files and directories on a different drive are available.

Follow these steps to look at the files on another drive:

1. Double-click the File Manager icon in the Main group window.

2. If necessary, insert a floppy disk in your floppy drive.

3. Click the appropriate drive icon on the drive bar.

   or

   WfW

   Open the drive list by clicking the underlined arrow next to the list. Select the drive from the list.

   or

   Pull down the **D**isk menu and choose **S**elect Drive. Select the drive from the Select Drive dialog box.

   Note: *Instead of following step 3, you can press Ctrl plus the drive letter. This method works even if the drive bar is not displayed.*

The directory window now contains a list of files and directories for a disk in the floppy drive.

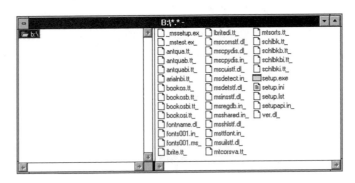

Task: Open Multiple Directory Windows

File Manager can display multiple windows simultaneously to show the file contents of any drive, directory, or subdirectory you select. Open multiple directory windows for different disks and directories to make comparing disk contents or copying and deleting files easier. See Lesson 8, "Managing Files, Directories, and Disks," for more information on copying and deleting files.

Follow these steps to open multiple directory windows:

1. Double-click the File Manager icon in the Main group window.

2. Notice which drive is currently displayed.

3. Double-click a different drive icon on the drive bar to open a new window with information on that drive.

   Note: *A single click on a drive icon displays information in the existing directory window. A double-click on a drive icon opens a new directory window for the information.*

Task: Arrange Multiple Directory Windows

You can arrange directory windows in three ways. You can arrange them by cascading them to show all the window titles or by tiling them to show each window's contents. Or, if you are working with many directory windows, you might want to reduce the windows to icons at the bottom of the File Manager window.

Follow these steps to arrange directory windows in a cascade:

1. Double-click the File Manager icon in the Main group window.

2. Open two or more directory windows.

3. Pull down the **W**indow menu and choose **C**ascade.

The active window becomes the top window in the cascade.

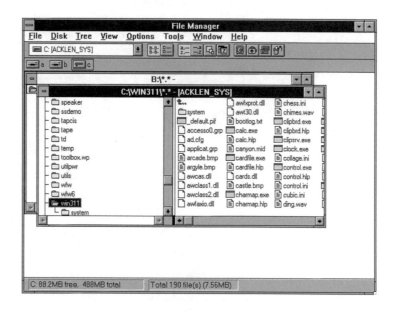

7

Follow these steps to arrange directory windows in tiles:

1. Double-click the File Manager icon in the Main group window.

2. Open two or more directory windows.

3. Pull down the **W**indow menu and choose Tile **H**orizontally or **T**ile Vertically.

File Manager displays horizontally tiled windows with the active window at the top.

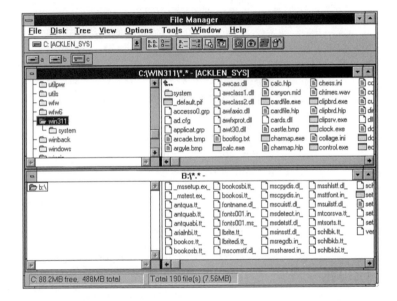

File Manager displays vertically tiled windows with the active window on the left.

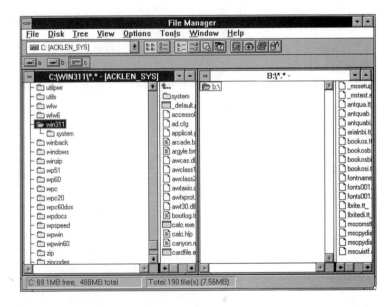

To make a directory window active, click anywhere in the window. If you can't see a directory window, move the active window to the side. After you arrange windows by cascading or tiling, you can size the windows manually. Lesson 2, "Working with Windows," describes how to move and size a window.

The third method for arranging directory windows is to reduce them to icons. Follow these steps to reduce a directory window to an icon:

1. Double-click the File Manager icon in the Main group window.

2. Click the Minimize button (down arrow) in the upper-right corner of the title bar.

If you have problems...

If you don't see a down arrow in the upper-right corner of the title bar, your directory window is maximized. Restore the window by clicking the Restore button (up and down arrows) in the upper-right corner; then click the Minimize button.

The path name of each directory window is displayed below the icon.

Minimized icons

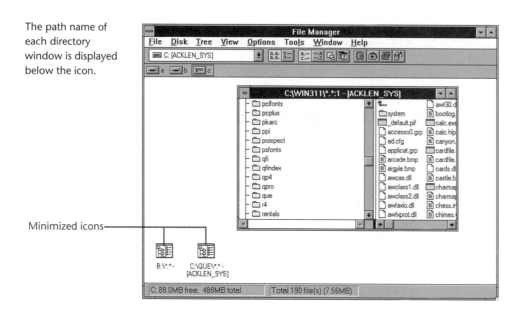

Note: *You can restore a directory icon to a directory window by double-clicking the icon.*

Task: Search for Files

Losing a file is frustrating and wastes time. With Windows, you can search drives or directories for a file name pattern to help locate the file you have misplaced.

To search for a file by its name or part of its name, follow these steps:

1. Double-click the File Manager icon in the Main group window.

2. Select the drive you want to search.

3. Select the directory (if you want to search a single directory).

   If you are not sure of the specific directory that contains a file, select the parent directory of all subdirectories that might contain the file.

4. Pull down the **F**ile menu and choose the Sear**ch** command.

5. In the **S**earch For text box, type the name of the file for which you are searching. You can include DOS wild-card characters in the file name.

6. To search all directories on the current drive, specify the root directory in the Start **F**rom text box. To search through all files on drive C, for example, type **C:** in the text box.

You can use a file name pattern to search for files in the Search dialog box.

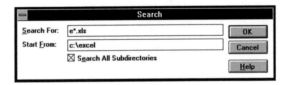

By default, Windows searches all subdirectories below the directory you select. To search only the specified directory, turn off the Se**a**rch All Subdirectories option.

7. Click OK.

The Search Results window displays the paths and file names of all files that match the pattern for which you were looking.

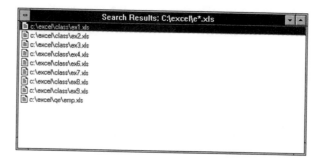

DOS wild-card characters are especially helpful when you search for files. The wild-card * stands for any combination of one or more characters, and the wild card ? stands for any one character. The following table shows examples of their uses:

Example	Description
e*.xls	Searches for all files whose names begin with an E and end with the extension XLS
bdgt???.xls	Searches for all files whose names begin with BDGT followed by any three characters and end with the extension XLS
taylor.*	Searches for all files whose names consist of TAYLOR and end with any extension
*.ltr	Searches for all files whose names contain any characters and end with the extension LTR

If you know the directory in which a file is located and the date or time the file was last saved, but don't know the file name, you can display the date and time of all files in the directory window; this display might help you locate the file. Pull down the **V**iew menu and choose **A**ll File Details to show the date and time the files were last saved. You can also sort a list of files by this date and time information. The following section contains more information on sorting a file list.

7

Task: Sort a File List

Locating files can be easier when you reorganize the contents of a directory window. By default, File Manager lists files and directories alphabetically by name, but you can order the window contents alphabetically by file extension, file size, or the date the file was last saved.

Note that files and directories are sorted separately. If you sort by date, the directories will be sorted by date and displayed at the top of the list. Then the files, sorted by date, will appear below the directories. Files and directories are never intermixed in the contents list.

Sorting by type can make files easier to find.

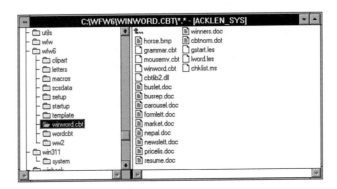

Sorting by date distinguishes older files from newer ones.

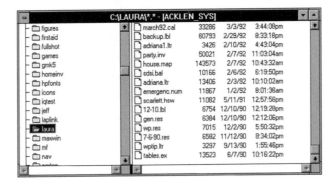

To sort a window's contents by file name, file extension, file size, or file date, follow these steps:

1. Double-click the File Manager icon in the Main group window.

2. Activate the directory window you want to sort.

3. Pull down the **V**iew menu and choose one of these options:

Command	Description
Sort by Name	Sorts the display alphabetically by file name
Sort **b**y Type	Sorts the display alphabetically by file extension and then by file name
Sort by Si**z**e	Sorts by file size, from largest to smallest
Sort by **D**ate	Sorts by last date saved, from newest to oldest

Note: *You do not have to display the file date or size in the directory window to sort by those attributes.*

Exploring File Manager's Toolbar

WfW

Windows 3.11 for Workgroups added a toolbar to File Manager to make common tasks easier to accomplish. Instead of locating and selecting a command from the menu, you can click a button on the toolbar. Table 7.2 illustrates and describes the toolbar buttons.

Table 7.2 File Manager Toolbar Buttons		
Button Name	**Button**	**Description**
Connect Network Drive		Connects to a shared directory
Disconnect Network Drive		Disconnects from a shared directory
Share As		Sets up a directory to be shared with other users on your network
Stop Sharing		Resets a shared directory so that it can no longer be accessed by other users on the network
File Names		Displays only the names of each file
All File Detail		Displays all the file details

7

(continues)

Table 7.2 Continued		
Button Name	**Button**	**Description**
Sort By Name		Displays files in alphabetic order by file name
Sort By Type		Displays files in alphabetic order by file extension
Sort By Size		Displays files in order of size, largest to smallest
Sort By Date		Displays files in chronological order by date
Run Microsoft Backup		Runs the Microsoft Backup for Windows program that comes with DOS 6.2
Run Microsoft Anti-Virus		Runs the Microsoft Anti-Virus for Windows program that comes with DOS 6.2
Compression Information		Runs the DOS 6.2 Doublespace Information program
Run Microsoft Undelete		Runs the Microsoft Undelete for Windows program that comes with DOS 6.2
Send Mail		Starts the Mail program so that you can send the selected file as an attachment to a message

Note: *If you install DOS 6.2 after you install Windows for Workgroups, the DOS installation program automatically adds the DOS 6.2 tool buttons to the File Manager toolbar.*

If you are not running DOS 6.2 or later, you will not have the toolbar buttons for those tools. If you are not on a network, you will not have the network drive and drive-sharing tools. File Manager's network tools are discussed in more detail in Lesson 9, "Working with Network Drives."

The toolbar can be customized to suit your specific needs. You can remove buttons you will not use, and you can add those you will use frequently. To customize your toolbar, choose Customize Tool**b**ar from the **O**ptions menu.

Task: Create a File Association

One of the convenient features of Windows is its capacity to start a program when you choose an *associated* document. When you choose an associated document, Windows starts the associated program and then loads that document. The extension of the file is used to associate a file with a program. In fact, when you create a file association, you associate all the files with a particular extension with a certain program.

Many Windows programs create associations for their own files by modifying the Windows WIN.INI file when the program is installed. For example, all files with a WRI extension are associated with the Write program, and all files with a DOC extension are associated with Word for Windows.

You can add associations of your own to fit your programs and work habits. For example, you might want to associate all LTR files with your word processing program, or all BAT files with the Microsoft Editor program.

Here are some programs and their common document file extensions:

Program	Extensions
Microsoft Excel	XLS, XLC, and XLM
Microsoft Word for Windows	DOC and DOT
WordPerfect for Windows	WPD
Paintbrush	BMP
Write	WRI
Lotus 1-2-3	WKS and WK1

7

To associate a document file with a specific program, follow these steps:

1. Double-click the File Manager icon in the Main group window.

2. Select the directory containing the data file (document file) you want to associate with a program.

3. Select the name of the file you want associated. Windows associates document files with programs by checking the file extension of the document file.

4. Pull down the **F**ile menu and choose the **A**ssociate command.

The Associate dialog
box appears.

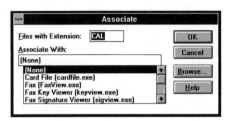

Note: *Some Windows programs automatically translate or convert data
documents from other programs. For example, Lotus 1-2-3 files can be
associated with the Excel program.*

5. Scroll through the list box attached to the **A**ssociate With text box
to find the name of the program to be associated with files that
have the extension shown in the **F**iles with Extension box. Select
the program name if you find it. If you do not find the program
name, proceed to the next step.

6. If you do not find the program name in the **A**ssociate With list,
type the full path and file name of the program file in the **A**ssociate
With text box. If you are not sure of the correct directory path or
file name, you can search for it by clicking the **B**rowse button.

7. Click OK.

Some DOS programs, such as WordPerfect 5.1+, can use any file extension for their data documents. In that case, you must associate each of
the different file extensions that you use with WordPerfect with that
program.

**If you have
problems...**

Some DOS programs may not start directly from an associated file; some
programs may start but not run as efficiently as they should. If this is true for
the document files you are using, refer to Lesson 13, "Installing and Configuring DOS Applications," for information on creating a PIF.

Task: Start Programs from File Manager

You can use Program Manager to group together a frequently used program and an associated document so that they are readily accessible. On some occasions, however, the program you want to start may not be in a group window. When this happens, start the program from File Manager (you can start any program from File Manager).

Follow these steps to start a program from File Manager:

1. Double-click the File Manager icon in the Main group window.

2. Select the drive and directory where the program file is located.

You can double-click a program file in File Manager to start the program.

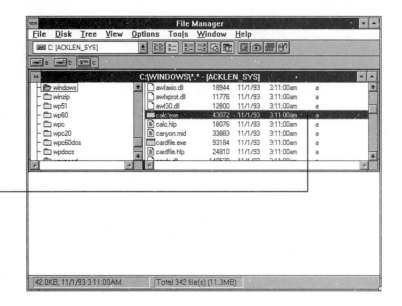

Double-click here to start the Calculator program

3. Double-click the program file.

Most program file names end with EXE or COM. You may have to start some DOS programs by double-clicking a file with the extension BAT or PIF, as described in Lesson 13, "Installing and Configuring DOS Applications."

You can associate document files or data files so that they start a particular program. Choosing this associated document or data file starts the program and also loads the document or data.

7

Summary

To	Do This
Start File Manager	Open the Main group window. Double-click the File Manager icon.
View the contents of a directory	Double-click the File Manager icon in the Main group window. Click the directory name.
Display specific file information	Double-click the File Manager icon in the Main group window. If necessary, select the directory window. Pull down the **V**iew menu and choose **A**ll File Details, **P**artial Details, or **B**y File Type.
Expand a directory	Double-click the File Manager icon in the Main group window. Double-click the closed directory icon.
Collapse a directory	Double-click the File Manager icon in the Main group window. Double-click the open directory icon.
Change to a different drive	Double-click the File Manager icon in the Main group window. Click the drive icon on the drive bar. Or select the drive from the Drive drop-down list on the toolbar. Or pull down the **D**isk menu and choose **S**elect Drive.
Open multiple directory windows	Double-click the File Manager icon in the Main group window. Double-click a drive icon on the drive bar.
Cascade multiple directory windows	Double-click the File Manager icon in the Main group window. Open two or more directory windows. Pull down the **W**indow menu and choose **C**ascade.
Tile multiple directory windows	Double-click the File Manager icon in the Main group window. Open two or more directory windows. Pull down the **W**indow menu and choose Tile **H**orizontally or Tile **V**ertically.
Minimize a directory window to an icon	Double-click the File Manager icon in the Main group window. Click the Minimize button in the directory window. If the directory window is maximized, restore the window first.

To	Do This
Search for files	Double-click the File Manager icon in the Main group window. Select the drive and directory you want to search. Pull down the File menu and choose Search. Type the name of the file or a file name pattern, including wild-card characters, in the Search For text box. If necessary, specify the directory to search in the Start From text box.
Sort a file list	Double-click the File Manager icon in the Main group window. Display in the contents list the list of files you want to sort. Pull down the View menu and choose one of the four sorting options: Sort by Name, Sort by Type, Sort by Size, and Sort by Date.
Use the File Manager toolbar	Double-click the File Manager icon in the Main group window. Click a button on the toolbar to execute the frequently used menu command the button represents.
Create a file association	Double-click the File Manager icon in the Main group window. Select the file you want associated with a program. Pull down the File menu and choose Associate. Select the name of the program in the Associate With text box. If you cannot find the program name, type the full path (drive, directory, and file name) for the program file in the Associate With text box. If you cannot remember the name or location of the file, click Browse to look for it.
Start a program from File Manager	Double-click the File Manager icon in the Main group window. Locate the program file in the contents list. Double-click the file name.

7

On Your Own
Estimated time: 20 minutes

1. Start File Manager and display a list of files for the Windows directory.

2. Display all file details for the Windows directory.

3. Display only the file name, modification date, and modification time.

4. Navigate through your list of directories, expanding and collapsing different directories.

5. Open another directory window for a different drive (another local hard drive, a floppy drive, or a network drive if available).

6. Open a total of three directory windows. Tile the windows horizontally. Move among the directory windows.

7. Search for all files on your hard disk with the extension SYS.

8. Sort a file list first by date, then by file size.

9. Practice starting a program from File Manager by starting the Calculator program in the Window directory.

Lesson 8

Managing Files, Directories, and Disks

Working without a hard disk can be difficult, but working *with* one can be confusing. Problems arise if people don't erase unnecessary files or don't make backup copies of files in case the hard drive fails.

This lesson shows how easily you can erase unwanted files, copy files to other disks, and move files between directories. You learn also how to make your own directories so that you can organize your hard disk to fit your work and data.

Specifically, this lesson teaches you how to

- Create valid file names and directory names
- Select files and directories
- Copy files and directories
- Move files and directories
- Use drag-and-drop techniques to move and copy files and directories
- Rename files and directories
- Delete files and directories
- Create a directory
- Format a floppy disk

■ Copy a floppy disk

■ Identify MS-DOS tools in File Manager

Understanding File Names

File names and directory names have rules you must follow if you want to find your data again. If you do not name a file or directory correctly, you may not be able to find it later, or the name may not be accepted.

File names and directory names have three parts:

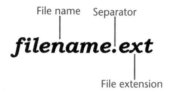

The file name (or directory name) can contain from one to eight characters. The separator is always a period. The file extension is optional and can have as many as three characters. In most cases, Windows programs add their own file extensions to the file names you type.

Note: *File names are not case sensitive. In other words, ABCDEFGH.IJK is the same as abcdefgh.ijk.*

For file names and directory names, you can use any of the alphabetic and numeric characters, as well as the following symbols across the top of the keyboard:

! @ # $ % ^ & ( ) _ -

You should not use the asterisk (*), plus sign (+), equal sign (=), vertical bar (|), slash (/), brackets ([ ]), colon (:), semicolon (;), comma (,), quotation mark ("), greater than sign (>), less than sign (<) or backslash (\).

If you start a file name with a symbol, the name appears at the top of alphabetic lists of files (such as the list that appears in the Open dialog box). Starting file names with symbols is a good trick for files you use often and want to find quickly.

Note: *Never use a space in a file name or directory name. Include a period only if you are using a file extension.*

Copying, Moving, and Deleting Files and Directories

Select, then do
All Windows programs follow the technique of selecting an item (such as a file) and then taking action on it (such as choosing a command from a menu).

All Windows programs follow the same philosophy: *select, then do.* Before you can work on a file or directory, you must select it. In some cases— when copying or deleting files, for example—you may want to select multiple files before giving a single command.

Task: Select Files and Directories

You have several ways to select files and directories. If you can find the items you want in the list, you can use the mouse to select them. You may want to select a certain group of files, in which case you would use the **S**elect Files command. Multiple files and directories can be selected and treated as a group.

Follow these steps to select a single file or directory:

1. Double-click the File Manager icon in the Main group window.

2. If necessary, choose the correct drive.

3. Scroll through the list until you can see the file or directory in the list.

4. Click the file or directory name to select it.

Follow these steps to select multiple files or directories that are adjacent to each other:

1. Double-click the File Manager icon in the Main group window.

2. If necessary, choose the correct drive.

3. Scroll through the list until you can see all the files or directories in the list.

8

4. Click the first file or directory to select it.

5. Hold down the Shift key and then click the last file or directory. All the files or directories between the two selections will be selected.

In this example, eight files—totaling 110K, as indicated on the status bar—are selected.

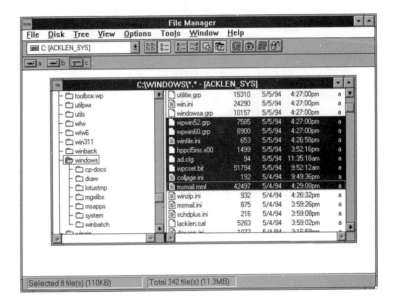

Follow these steps to select multiple files or directories that are not adjacent to each other:

1. Double-click the File Manager icon in the Main group window.

2. If necessary, choose the correct drive.

3. Scroll through the list until you can see the files or directories in the list.

4. Click the first file or directory to select it.

5. Hold down the Ctrl key and click the other files or directories.

If you have problems... If you accidentally select too many files, you can hold down the Ctrl key and click a file to deselect it.

This window shows
that seven
nonadjacent files
are selected.

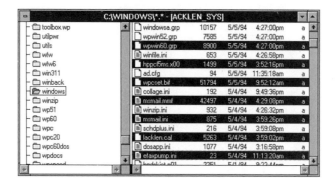

Follow these steps to select files by a file name pattern:

1. Double-click the File Manager icon in the Main group window.

2. If necessary, choose the correct drive.

3. Pull down the **F**ile menu and choose **S**elect Files.

In the Select Files
dialog box, you can
type a specific
extension and use
DOS wild-card
characters to select
a particular group
of files.

> **Note:** *To select all files in the window, click the **S**elect button while the **F**ile(s) box displays ***.***. Then click **C**lose to select all the files in the contents list.*

4. Type the file pattern in the **F**ile(s) text box. For example, to select all files with an XLS extension, type ***.xls**. See the section "Task: Search for Files" in Lesson 7 for more information on DOS wild cards and file patterns.

5. Click **S**elect.

> **Note:** *You can use the **D**eselect option to cancel the selection you specified in the **F**ile(s) text box.*

8

6. If necessary, type another file pattern to select another group of files.

7. Choose **C**lose.

Task: Copy a File or Directory

Copying files is an important part of keeping your work organized and secure. When organizing files, you may have to copy a file to make it accessible in two locations. A more important reason for copying files is security. The hard disk on which you store files is a mechanical device and has one of the highest failure rates among computer components. Should your hard disk fail, the cost of replacing the disk is insignificant compared to the cost of the hours you worked accumulating data on the disk. One way to prevent the loss of this data is to make a backup set of files on another drive (such as a floppy disk drive).

If you have ever used DOS commands to copy files and directories, you will find that copying is much easier with Windows and a mouse. All you do is drag the files or directories you want to copy from one location in the directory window to another location.

Follow these steps to copy files or directories:

1. Double-click the File Manager icon in the Main group window.

2. Make sure that both the source and destination are visible.

   The *source* is the item you want to copy. It can be a file icon in the contents list, or a directory icon from the contents list or directory tree.

   The *destination* can be a directory icon in the contents list or directory tree. The destination can also be a directory icon at the bottom of the File Manager window, or a disk icon at the top of the File Manager window.

3. Select the directory (or directories) and file (or files) you want to copy.

In the directory tree, you can select only a single directory or subdirectory to copy. In the contents list, however, you can select multiple files or subdirectories to copy simultaneously. When you copy a directory or subdirectory, you copy all the subdirectories and files it contains.

This example shows that several files are selected.

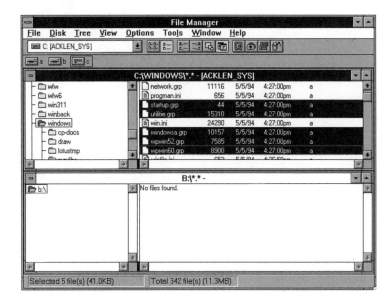

4. Pull down the **F**ile menu and choose **C**opy. Type the destination drive (and directory) in the **T**o text box. Click OK.

or

Drag the directory or file icon to the destination. If the destination is the same drive as the source, hold down the Ctrl key. If you do not hold down the Ctrl key, you will *move* the files.

Note: *When you are copying files or directories, the drag-and-drop icon will have a plus sign (+) in it.*

8

The selected files are dragged to the destination window.

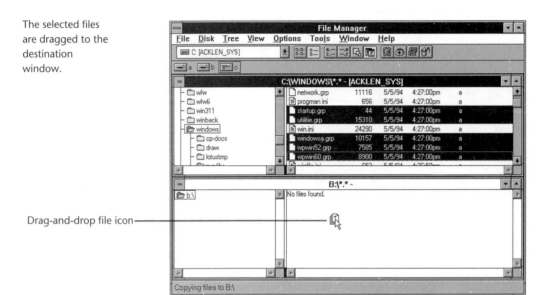

Drag-and-drop file icon

5. When the file icon is over the destination, release the mouse button; release the Ctrl key if you are using it.

Note: *If the destination is a drive icon, the files or directories will be copied to the current directory on the drive.*

6. File Manager displays a Confirm Mouse Operation dialog box and asks you to confirm the copy action.

If the destination has a file with the same name as the file you are copying, you are asked to confirm that the file at the destination can be replaced by the copy.

Task: Move a File or Directory

You can move files and directories just as easily as you can copy them. Moving files and directories puts them in a new location and removes the originals from the old location. Moving a directory moves that directory's files and subdirectories.

To move files or directories, follow these steps:

1. Double-click the File Manager icon in the Main group window.

2. Make both the source and destination visible.

The *source* is the item you want to copy. It can be a file icon in the contents list, or a directory icon in the contents list or directory tree.

The *destination* can be a directory icon in the directory tree or contents list. The destination can also be a directory icon at the bottom of the File Manager window, or a disk icon at the top of the File Manager window.

Caution

Never move a file in use in another program.

3. Select the files or directories you want to move.

4. Pull down the **F**ile menu and choose **M**ove. Type the destination drive (and directory) in the **T**o text box. Click OK.

or

Drag the file icon or directory icon to the destination if the destination is on the same disk. If the destination is on a different disk, press and hold down the Shift key as you drag. (If you do not press and hold down the Shift key, you *copy* the files rather than move them.)

Note: *When you are moving files or directories, the drag-and-drop icon will not show a plus sign (+) in it.*

5. When the file icon is over the destination, release the mouse button; release the Shift key if you are using it.

Note: *If the destination is a drive icon, the files or directories will be moved to the current directory on the drive.*

6. When you are asked to confirm the move, consider whether you are copying or moving and how the files will change. Then choose Yes to complete the action, No to stop a single move, or Cancel to cancel all moves.

Using Drag-and-Drop Techniques

Although there are menu commands to copy and move files, it is much easier to drag items to their destination with the mouse. That way, you don't have to remember long path names and type them *exactly* right, thereby saving time and frustration.

8

The following table summarizes the mouse actions you take to move or copy files with the mouse:

Action You Want to Take	Mouse Action
Copy to a different disk	Drag
Copy to the same disk	Ctrl+drag
Move to a different disk	Shift+drag
Move to the same disk	Drag

Task: Rename a File or Directory

Unless you do everything perfectly the first time, you will find times when you want to rename a file or directory.

Caution

Never rename a file in use in another program.

To rename a file or directory, follow these steps:

1. Select the file or directory from a directory window.

2. From the **F**ile menu, choose the Re**n**ame command.

You supply the new file or directory name in the Rename dialog box.

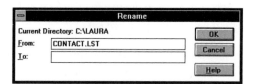

3. In the **T**o text box, type the new file name.

4. Click OK.

Note: *Renaming a directory is not the same as moving it. You can specify only a new directory name, not a new drive or parent directory.*

If you have problems...

If you enter a file name that already exists, a warning box appears after you click OK. You need to type a *unique* file name.

Task: Delete a File or Directory

You can delete files or directories when you want to remove old work from your disk. Deleting files makes more storage space available on the disk. Deleting directories that don't contain any files makes very little difference in storage space, but it does unclutter your directory tree.

Unless you have installed special software, you cannot recover files or directories after you delete them. Be very careful to select only the files or directories you want to delete. If you aren't sure about deleting files or directories, move them to a floppy disk instead. This is called *archiving* and can save you a lot of time and trouble if you discover that you needed the files after all.

Be careful that you do not accidentally select a directory when selecting files you want to delete. If you select a directory and choose **F**ile **D**elete, you delete all the files in the directory and the directory itself! Deleting entire directories can be convenient, but it can also be a real surprise if it is not what you intended to do.

To delete files or subdirectories, follow these steps:

1. Double-click the File Manager icon in the Main group window.

2. Select the files or directories you want to delete. Or you can use wild-card characters in step 4.

3. Pull down the **F**ile menu and choose **D**elete, or press Del.

4. If you have many files to delete, use DOS wild cards in the Delete text box.

Type ***.*** in the Delete text box to specify every file in the current directory.

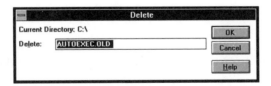

5. Click OK.

Confirm the deletion of the file(s) in the Confirm File Delete dialog box.

8

Note: *If you are deleting a directory, the Confirm Directory Delete dialog box will appear.*

6. Choose **Y**es, or choose Yes to **A**ll to confirm the deletion of several files at once.

Task: Create a Directory

Creating new directories on your disk is like adding new drawers to a filing cabinet. Creating new directories is an excellent way to reorganize or restructure your disk. After you build directories and subdirectories, you can put existing files in them with the **F**ile **M**ove and **F**ile **C**opy commands.

To make new directories, follow these steps:

1. Double-click the File Manager icon in the Main group window.

2. Select the drive or directory under which you want a new subdirectory.

3. Pull down the **F**ile menu and choose Cr**e**ate Directory.

Unless you specify otherwise, the new directory will be created under the Current Directory specified in the Create Directory dialog box.

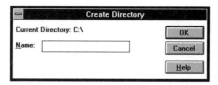

4. In the **N**ame text box, type the name of the new directory. Directory names follow the same rules as file names.

5. Click OK.

Adding new subdirectories is like growing new branches on a tree. New subdirectories must sprout from existing directories or subdirectories. If you want to create multiple layers of subdirectories, first create the directories or subdirectories that precede the ones you want to add.

Managing Floppy Disks

File Manager includes commands not only for copying files but also for copying entire floppy disks. You can copy one floppy to another—even if you have only a single disk drive. You can also use File Manager to format new floppy disks.

Task: Format a Floppy Disk

When you buy new floppy disks for storing data and files, you cannot use the disks until you format them (some disks come already formatted). Formatting prepares floppy disks for use by a specific type of computer. Part of the process of formatting is to check for bad areas on a disk's magnetic surface. If any bad areas are found, they are identified so that data is not recorded there.

Note: *If a floppy disk has data on it, formatting completely erases all existing data, which you cannot retrieve.*

To format a floppy disk, follow these steps:

1. Put the disk you want to format in the disk drive.

2. From the **D**isk menu, choose the **F**ormat Disk command.

Use the Format Disk dialog box to format and label disks.

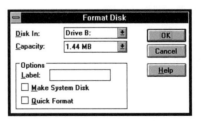

3. In the **D**isk In list box, select the disk drive containing the disk you want to format.

4. Select the appropriate disk size in the **C**apacity list box.

5. If you want to assign a label to the disk, type the label in the **L**abel text box.

   Note: *Label names follow the same rules as file names with one exception. File Manager will not let you enter a period separator. Type 1 to 11 characters without the period.*

8

6. Click **M**ake System Disk if you want to use the floppy disk to start your computer. Do not use this option unless it is needed, because the system files use storage space on the disk that can otherwise be used for data.

7. Click **Q**uick Format to save time if you are reasonably sure that the floppy disk does not have bad areas. You can use this option only if the disk has already been formatted.

8. Click OK. A message box warns you that formatting will erase all data on the floppy disk. If you are sure, choose **Y**es.

9. After the disk is formatted, you are given the chance to format additional disks.

It's a good idea to format an entire box of disks at one time and put a paper label on each formatted disk. That way, you know that open boxes contain formatted disks; paper labels confirm that the disks are formatted.

Task: Copy a Floppy Disk

Make duplicate copies of floppy disks whenever you need to store disk information off-site in a secure location or when you need to make a backup copy of original program disks.

To copy a floppy disk, follow these steps:

1. Double-click the File Manager icon in the Main group window.

2. Protect the original disk by attaching a write-protect tab (on 5 1/4-inch disks) or by sliding open the write-protect notch (on 3 1/2-inch disks).

3. Insert the original disk (the source disk) in the source disk drive.

4. Insert the disk to receive the copy (the destination disk) in the second disk drive. If you don't have a second disk drive, don't be concerned.

5. From the **D**isk menu, choose the **C**opy Disk command.

You specify the
drive letters for the
source and
destination drives in
the Copy Disk
dialog box.

6. In the **S**ource In list box in the Copy Disk dialog box, select the drive letter for the source drive.

7. In the **D**estination In list box, select the drive letter for the destination drive (even if it is the same as the source drive).

8. Click OK.

9. Choose **Y**es in the Confirm Copy Disk dialog box. You will be prompted to switch the source disk and destination disk in and out of the single drive.

The Confirm Copy
Disk dialog box
appears, warning
you that all
information will be
lost from the
destination disk.

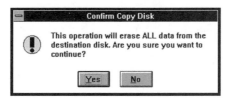

To use the **C**opy Disk command, you must have two floppy disks that are identical. For example, you cannot copy from a 3 1/2-inch disk that holds 1.4M of data to a 5 1/4-inch disk that holds 1.2M of data. To duplicate a disk, you must therefore use a destination disk with the same capacity as the source disk. File Manager prompts you to switch disks when necessary. Labeling your disks before you begin may help.

Notice that copying disks always completely erases the destination disk. Before you use the **C**opy Disk command, make sure that you will not be deleting important files from the destination disk. The **C**opy Disk command formats the destination disk if it is not already formatted.

8

Working with MS-DOS Tools

MS-DOS 6.0 and later includes Windows and DOS versions of Microsoft Anti-Virus, Microsoft Undelete, and Microsoft Backup. If you install MS-DOS 6.0 or 6.2 *after* you install Windows, the DOS installation program will add a Microsoft Tools group window with program icons for each of these three programs. If you are using Windows for Workgroups, the installation program will also add buttons for Anti-Virus, Backup, Undelete, and Doublespace Information to the File Manager toolbar. Finally, the installation program will add a Tools menu to the File Manager menu bar (in both Windows and Windows for Workgroups) with options for Backup, Anti-Virus, and Doublespace Information.

Note: *You can add the MS-DOS tools to Windows by using the steps in Lesson 3, "Working with Groups and Applications."*

This section provides a brief overview of the MS-DOS tools. For detailed information on using the tools, see *MS-DOS 6.2 QuickStart* or *Using MS-DOS 6.2*, Special Edition.

Microsoft Undelete

If you accidentally delete a file or group of files, you may be able to recover them with the Undelete program. When you delete a file, it is not physically deleted from the disk, only from the disk's directory. However, DOS marks the area as available free space, so the most important element in recovering deleted files is *not* to write to that disk. If you create or save another file to the disk, the file may be written to the area where your deleted file or files are stored.

You must act quickly to ensure the greatest chance of recovering deleted files from your disk. The Undelete program displays a list of files that can be successfully undeleted. If you choose to restore a deleted file, you will be asked to provide the first character in the file name.

Microsoft Backup

The most important measure you can take against data loss is to make backup copies of your data files. Although the Undelete program is very effective, it cannot recover all deleted files, especially if files have been written to the disk after the accidental deletion.

Your hard drive is a mechanical device and subject to failure, called a "disk crash." Replacing a hard disk is an inconvenience, but it does not compare to the task of re-creating all the data files you had stored on the drive. Creating a backup of your program and data files to floppy disks is your only protection against data loss from a disk crash.

The Backup program and its accompanying Restore program make it easy to create backup copies for select groups of files or for every file on your hard disk.

Microsoft Anti-Virus

Virus

A set of intentionally destructive instructions that can be copied to your hard drive from other sources, such as floppy disks and electronic bulletin boards.

Computer *viruses* are increasingly common; they are now found in all types of businesses. MS-DOS 6.0 and later includes two antivirus programs: Anti-Virus and VSafe. When you run Anti-Virus, it scans your system memory and the files on your disk drives to detect and clean off viruses. You can start the Anti-Virus program from the Microsoft Tools group window, the Tools menu in File Manager, or the Anti-Virus button on the File Manager toolbar.

The VSafe program is a TSR (terminate-and-stay-resident) program, which means that the program stays in memory after you run it. Because the program is loaded into memory, it can constantly monitor your system for viruses. If VSafe suspects that a virus is attempting to invade your system—from a floppy disk, for example— a warning message appears. When VSafe is running in memory, attempting to copy or open a file or disk containing a virus causes a warning dialog box to appear automatically. If your system's sound is turned on, you also may hear a special buzz or beep.

Summary

To	Do This
Select a single file or directory	Double-click the File Manager icon in the Main group window. Scroll through the list if necessary. Click the file or directory name.
Select adjacent files or directories	Double-click the File Manager icon in the Main group window. Scroll through the list if necessary. Click the first file or directory name. Hold down the Shift key and click the last file or directory name. All files and directories between the two files (or directories) will be selected.

8

(continues)

To	Do This
Select nonadjacent files or directories	Double-click the File Manager icon in the Main group window. Scroll through the list if necessary. Click the first file or directory name. Hold down the Ctrl key and click the other file names or directory names.
Copy a file or directory	Double-click the File Manager icon in the Main group window. Scroll through the list if necessary. Select the file or directory. Drag the file or directory to the destination drive (and directory). If the source and destination are the same drive, hold down the Ctrl key before you drag; or pull down the **F**ile menu and choose **C**opy. Type the destination drive and directory in the **T**o text box and click OK.
Move a file or directory	Double-click the File Manager icon in the Main group window. Scroll through the list if necessary. Select the file or directory. Drag the file or directory to the destination drive (and directory). If the source and destination are on different drives, hold down the Shift key before you drag; or pull down the **F**ile menu and choose **M**ove. Type the destination drive and directory in the **T**o text box and click OK.
Delete a file or directory	Double-click the File Manager icon in the Main group window. Select the file(s) or directory you want to delete. Pull down the **F**ile menu and choose **D**elete, or press Delete. Choose **Y**es or Yes to **A**ll to confirm the deletion of multiple files.
Create a directory	Double-click the File Manager icon in the Main group window. Select the drive or directory where you want to create the new directory. Pull down the **F**ile menu and choose Cr**e**ate Directory. Type the name of the new directory in the **N**ame text box and click OK.
Format a floppy disk	Double-click the File Manager icon in the Main group window. Pull down the **D**isk menu and choose **F**ormat Disk. In the **D**isk In list box, select the drive containing the disk you want to format. Select the appropriate size in the **C**apacity list box. Click OK and choose **Y**es in the confirmation dialog box.
Copy a floppy disk	Double-click the File Manager icon in the Main group window. Pull down the **D**isk menu and choose **C**opy Disk. Insert the source and destination disks in the drives. The drives must be of the same capacity. If you have only one drive, insert the source disk first. Choose the drive letter for the source and destination drives (even if they are the same). Click OK and choose **Y**es in the confirmation dialog box.

On Your Own
Estimated time: 20 minutes

1. Start File Manager. Display the list of files in the Windows directory.

2. Select seven adjacent files.

3. Select five nonadjacent files.

4. Select three adjacent directories in the contents list.

5. Make a backup copy of an important file onto a floppy disk. First format the floppy disk, if necessary.

6. Practice creating directories and moving files by reorganizing one of your directories into several subdirectories.

8

Lesson 9

Working with Network Drives

 If you are working with Windows for Workgroups, you can connect to shared directories on other computers on your network. Likewise, you can designate directories on your hard disk as shared so that other users can access the files in those directories. You use File Manager to connect to shared directories and to share directories on your computer.

In this lesson, you learn how to

- Connect to a shared directory
- Disconnect from a shared directory
- Share a directory
- Display a list of users for a shared directory
- Stop sharing a directory

Note: *The topics discussed in this lesson are applicable only to Windows for Workgroups.*

Network Access and Security

If you want to use network drives with Windows, you must log on to the network before you start Windows. See your network administrator for the procedure on how to log on to your network. When you connect your computer to a network, additional disk drives may be available. You can use any of these drives with Windows if you know the path name to the drive and the password.

One of the main functions of network software is to provide security for network drives. When network resources are shared, a security system must be designed to limit access to confidential information and to prevent unauthorized modification of important files.

In Windows for Workgroups, security is provided by the assignment of passwords and access rights. Only those directories specifically designated to be shared are visible to network users. Both network drives and local drives can be designated as shared drives.

Accessing a Shared Directory

You can connect to any directory that has been designated as shared by any user on your network (to learn how to share directories, see the section "Sharing Directories" later in this lesson). You use File Manager to connect to a directory.

Shared directory
A directory that can be shared by users connected to a local area network (LAN).

Network drive
A drive made available to you through a connection to a local area network.

When you connect to a *shared directory*, File Manager assigns a drive letter to that directory (or you can assign the drive letter of your choice). This creates a *network drive* for that directory.

Note: *It is important to understand the terminology used here. Although you are connecting to a certain shared* directory, *Windows for Workgroups treats that directory as a* network drive—*hence, the Connect Network Drive and Disconnect Network Drive buttons and commands.*

You can view the files in the directory by selecting the drive icon assigned to that directory or by selecting the drive from the drive list in the toolbar. You open files in the directory in exactly the same way you open a file on your hard disk. Whether you can modify the file depends on the level of access the owner of the directory has granted to other users.

Task: Connect to a Shared Directory

As a workgroup member, you can connect to any shared directory that you have access to in your workgroup. A minimum of read-only access is required to connect to the directory. A password may be required; if you enter an invalid password or don't know the password, you will not be able to access the directory.

Note: *A shared directory can be located on any computer connected to the Windows for Workgroups network.*

Follow these steps to connect to a shared directory:

1. Open File Manager.

2. Click the Connect Network Drive button on the toolbar.

Use the Connect Network Drive dialog box to select the computer and directory to which you want to connect.

3. By default, File Manager assigns the next available drive letter on your computer to the directory you select. To assign a different letter, open the **Drive** list (click the underlined down arrow) and select a letter from the list.

4. If you know the path of the shared directory, type it in the Path list box. The path includes the computer name where the directory is located, as well as the share name assigned to that directory. The computer name is preceded by double backslashes and is separated from the share name by a single backslash (for example, \\SALESMAN\SALES).

or

Open the **Path** drop-down list (click the underlined down arrow) and click a path from a list of recently used paths.

5. If you want to have this directory available whenever you use Windows for Workgroups, click Reconnect at Startup.

6. Click OK.

9

Network disk drive icons

Network drives
show up in File
Manager with
special network disk
drive icons.

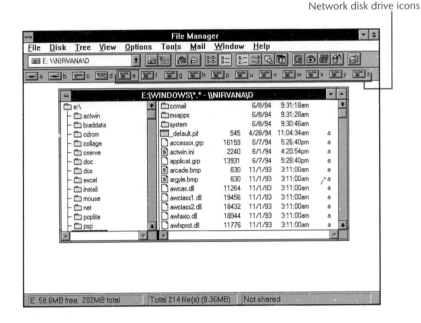

If you have problems...

If, when you attempt to connect to a shared directory, you get an error message stating that the drive letter you have chosen is invalid, you may not have any drive letters available to assign to the directory. The LASTDRIVE statement in your CONFIG.SYS file (stored in the root directory of your local hard drive) determines how many drive letters you can use. Use Windows Notepad (or any other text editor) to open the file. The LASTDRIVE command will have a drive letter, such as F, specified. Change the letter to a later letter in the alphabet (such as J), save the file, exit Windows, and reboot the computer.

By default, you have access to shared directories on your own computer. If you attempt to connect to a shared directory on your local drive, you will receive an error message. You can connect only to shared directories on other machines on the network.

Task: Disconnect from a Shared Directory

You may want to disconnect from a shared directory when you are finished with the files. Or, if you are connected to a shared directory on someone else's computer and you know that person will be turning the computer off, you should disconnect from that drive.

Follow these steps to disconnect from a shared directory:

1. Open File Manager.

2. Click the Disconnect Network Drive button on the toolbar.

You use the
Disconnect
Network Drive
dialog box to
disconnect from a
shared directory.

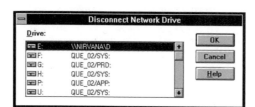

3. In the **Drive** list, double-click the drive from which you want to disconnect.

   You can select additional directories from the list if you want to disconnect from more than one directory at once. To select more than one directory, click the first directory, hold down the Ctrl key, and click subsequent directories. To deselect a directory, hold down the Ctrl key and click the directory.

4. Click OK.

Sharing Directories

When you enable other users to share your directories, you must decide what level of security you want to assign to that directory. Windows for Workgroups provides three levels of access rights:

■ *Full* allows a user to create, modify, delete, rename, move, and read files, as well as run applications. Users have complete access to all files in the directory.

■ *Read-Only* enables a user to open and view documents but not modify or delete a document. Read-Only access is all you need to run a program.

■ *Depends on Password* assigns either Full access or Read-Only access to the user, depending on the password the user uses.

   Note: *If you don't assign a password with Depends on Password access, anyone on the network can access your shared directory.*

9

*Note: You don't have to select **D**epends on Password to assign a password. You can select **R**ead-Only or **F**ull and still assign a password.*

The **D**epends on Password option allows you to assign both Full access and Read-Only access to the same directory. You assign a different password to each access level. If the user enters the password for Read-Only access, Windows for Workgroups enables access to that directory on a read-only basis. If the user enters the password for Full access, complete access to the directory is granted.

A share name must be specified when you set up a shared directory. This name appears in the list of shared directories for a certain computer in the workgroup. If necessary, you can assign a comment to provide additional information about the directory.

Task: Share a Directory

You can designate any directory on your computer as shared. Your computer must be turned on and logged on to the network in order for other users to access the shared directory.

Note: *You can use these steps also to change the share name, password, or comment for your shared directory.*

Follow these steps to share a directory:

1. Open File Manager.

2. Click the name of the directory you want to share.

3. Click the Share As button on the toolbar.

You use the Share Directory dialog box to share a directory on your computer.

```
┌─────────────────────────────────────────────────────┐
│  ═                  Share Directory                  │
├─────────────────────────────────────────────────────┤
│  Share Name:  │WINDOWS│                    ┌──────┐  │
│                                            │  OK  │  │
│  Path:        C:\WINDOWS                    └──────┘  │
│                                            ┌──────┐  │
│  Comment:     [                        ]   │Cancel│  │
│                                            └──────┘  │
│               ☒ Re-share at Startup        ┌──────┐  │
│                                            │ Help │  │
│  ┌─Access Type:──────────────────────┐    └──────┘  │
│  │ ○ Read-Only                        │              │
│  │ ⦿ Full                             │              │
│  │ ○ Depends on Password              │              │
│  └────────────────────────────────────┘             │
│  ┌─Passwords:──────────────────────────┐            │
│  │ Read-Only Password:   [          ]   │            │
│  │                                      │            │
│  │ Full Access Password: [          ]   │            │
│  └──────────────────────────────────────┘           │
└─────────────────────────────────────────────────────┘
```

4. The name of the directory you selected in step 2 is the default name of the shared directory. You can type a new name in the Share Name text box.

5. The path of the directory you selected in step 2 appears in the Path text box. If you selected the wrong directory in step 2, type the path for the correct directory.

6. You can type a comment in the Comment text box. This can be helpful when other users are looking for a particular shared directory to connect to.

7. If you want to reshare automatically the directory at startup, click Re-share at Startup.

8. Select an access level in the Access Type area. The choices are Read-only, Full, and Depends on Password.

If you want to limit access to the files in the shared directory to certain users, assign a password to the directory and give the password to only those users. If you select the Depends on Password option, you need to enter two passwords, one for users who have read-only access to your files and one for users with full access. If you want all users to have access to your files, don't assign a password.

9. Type a password in one or both of the Read-Only Password and Full Access Password boxes, depending on which option you selected in step 8. Click OK.

You use the Confirm Password Change dialog box to verify old passwords and enter new ones.

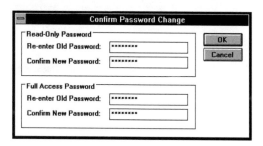

10. To confirm passwords, enter old and new passwords in text boxes that are enabled.

9

11. Click OK. The directory's folder icon changes to a hand holding a folder, indicating that the directory is now shared.

Task: Display a List of Users for a Shared Directory

If you are sharing your local directories with other users, you may want to know which directories are being used by other users at any time, or you may want to know which users are using specific files. For example, if someone else is using one of your files in your local shared directory, you may want to warn that person if you need to turn off your computer. Some files will restrict the access or capabilities of other users while the files are being shared. In that case, you may want to ask the user to stop using the file so that another user can have full access.

Note: *You can display a list of users for only* your *shared directories. If another user has shared a directory, you will not be able to display a list of users for that directory.*

Follow these steps to display a list of users for a shared directory (or file):

1. Open File Manager.

2. Click the directory or file you want to check.

3. Pull down the File menu and choose Properties.

4. Click Open By to display the Open Files dialog box. This button appears only if you have selected a shared directory or file.

The Open Files dialog box shows the sharing status of files in a selected directory.

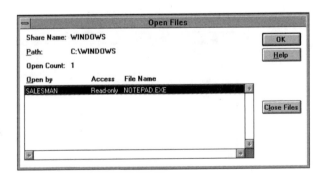

The Network Properties dialog box shows the sharing status of a selected file.

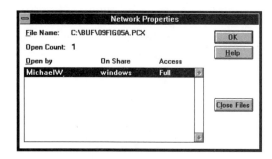

5. Click OK twice to return to the directory window.

Caution

If you stop sharing a directory while other users are using its files, the users may lose data. Stop sharing only after you have notified all users.

You use the Stop Sharing dialog box to select the directories you want to stop sharing.

Task: Stop Sharing a Directory

You can stop sharing a directory at any time if you no longer want other users to have access to it.

Note: *You will have to stop sharing a directory before you can delete or move it.*

To stop sharing a directory, follow these steps:

1. Open File Manager.

2. Click the Stop Sharing button on the toolbar.

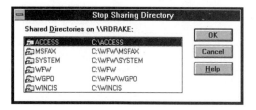

3. In the Shared Directories On list, click the name of the directory you want to stop sharing.

   You can select additional directories from the list if you want to stop sharing more than one directory at once. To select more than one directory, click the first directory, hold down the Ctrl key, and click subsequent directories. To deselect a directory, hold down the Ctrl key and click the directory.

4. Click OK.

9

5. If other people are working in the directory you want to stop sharing, a confirmation dialog box will appear. If you choose Yes, these people may lose their data.

Summary

To	Do This
Connect to a shared directory	Open File Manager. Click the Connect Network Drive button on the toolbar. Specify the path of the directory you want to connect to. Click OK.
Disconnect from a shared directory	Open File Manager. Click the Disconnect Network Drive button. In the **Drive** list, double-click the drive from which you want to disconnect, and click OK. Or click the first drive name, hold down Ctrl, click subsequent drive names, and then click OK.
Share a directory	Open File Manager. Click the name of the directory you want to share. Click the Share As button on the toolbar. If necessary, correct the name and path of the directory and type a comment for the directory. Select an access level. If necessary, type a password for one or both access levels. Click OK.
Display a list of users for a shared directory	Open File Manager. Click the directory or file you want to check. Pull down the **File** menu and choose Properties. Click **Open** By. Click OK twice to return to the directory window.
Stop sharing a directory	Open File Manager. Click the Stop Sharing button on the toolbar. Click the name(s) of the directory you want to stop sharing in the Shared Directories On list. Click OK.

On Your Own
Estimated time: 10 minutes

1. Connect to a shared directory on your network.

2. View a list of users for a shared directory.

3. Disconnect from the shared directory.

4. Set up a directory on your system as a shared directory.

5. Stop sharing the directory.

Part IV
Working with Windows Applications

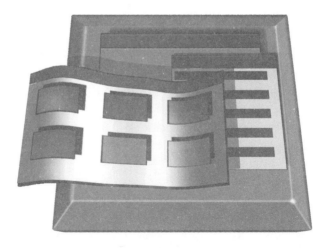

Lesson 10

Using Write

Write is a word processing program that comes with Windows. It is simple to use but powerful enough to accomplish common word processing tasks. The concepts you learn while using Write also apply to more powerful Windows word processing programs, such as Microsoft Word for Windows and WordPerfect for Windows.

In this lesson, you learn how to

- Start and exit Write
- Type and edit text
- Move around in a Write document
- Find and replace text
- Enhance text
- Save and open files
- Print a document

Creating a Write Document

To start Write, you must first start Windows. (Refer to Lesson 1, "Learning the Basics," if you need help starting Windows.) Windows Write is a Windows word processing program located in the Accessories program group.

When the Accesso-
ries window is
open, Write appears
as an icon with its
name below the
icon.

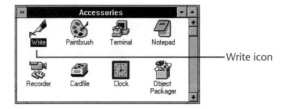

Write icon

Follow these steps to start the Write program:

1. Open the Accessories group window.

2. Locate the Write icon, scrolling through the group window if necessary.

3. Double-click the Write icon.

When you first
open Write, a new
window appears,
containing a blank
Write document.

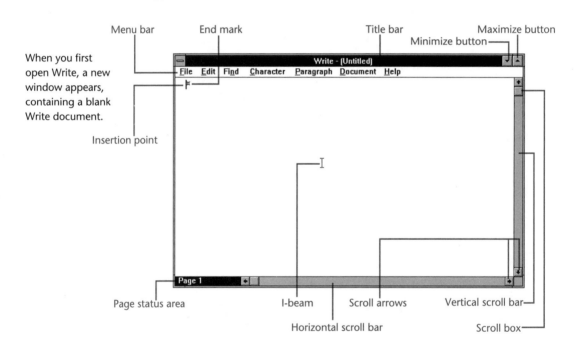

Some parts of the Write window are like other windows. A title bar across
the top displays the name of the program and the name of the document
(Untitled until you name it). A menu bar is below the title bar, and scroll
bars are at the right and bottom of the window.

Besides having these familiar window parts, Write has some unique features: an *insertion point* where characters appear as you type; an *end mark* that shows the end of your typing; and a *page status area* at the bottom-left corner of the window. The mouse pointer may appear as an arrow (over a menu name or a scroll bar or in the left margin) or as an I-beam (in the typing area of the screen).

Task: Type a Sample Document

Word wrap
A feature that causes text to move down to the next line when the current line is full.

When you start Write, you open a new Write document. You are then ready to start typing. Like all word processing programs, Write offers *word wrap*, a feature that enables you to type to the right margin and just keep typing. As you type, the text automatically wraps down to the next line. When you get to the end of a paragraph, press Enter. (Press Enter twice to leave a blank line between paragraphs.)

Each character you type appears at the blinking insertion point, pushing the insertion point one character to the right. The end mark stays at the bottom of the document.

To type a short letter, follow these steps:

1. Open Write.

2. Type the current date in the upper-left corner of the blank document.

3. Press Enter four times to space down for the address.

4. Type the address shown in the accompanying figure, pressing Enter at the end of each line.

The sample letter
with the current
date and inside
address.

Current date

Three blank lines
between the date
and the address

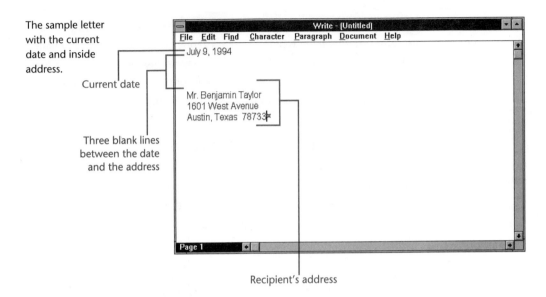

Recipient's address

5. Press Enter twice to insert a blank line between the address and the salutation.

6. Type the salutation and then press Enter twice to insert a blank line between the salutation and the body of the letter.

7. Type the body of the letter as shown in the next figure. Press Enter twice at the end of each paragraph in the body of the letter.

   Note: *Be sure that you don't press Enter until you reach the end of a paragraph. Press Enter twice to insert a blank line between paragraphs.*

8. Type **Sincerely,** and press Enter four times to insert three blank lines between the closing and the signature line.

9. Type your full name on the signature line and press Enter.

10. Type **Customer Service Representative** as the second signature line.

In this example, the top part of the sample letter has scrolled off the screen.

Body text

Closing

Three blank lines between the closing and the signature line

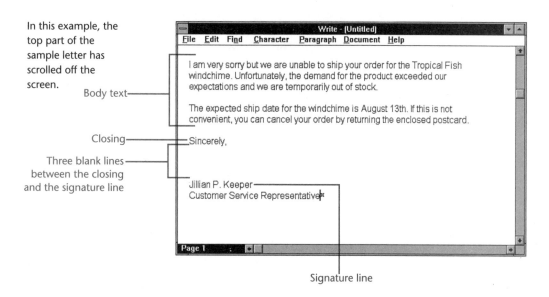

Signature line

| **If you have problems...** | If your computer screen is not wide enough to show the full document width, the typing area may be wider than the screen. In that case, the screen scrolls left and right as you type, attempting to show you each word typed. If you find the scrolling annoying, consider making the window larger (see the section "Task: Resize a Window" in Lesson 2). |

Moving Around in a Document

Because one of the biggest advantages of a word processing program is its capability to edit text, you need to know how to move around on the screen to locate the text you want to edit. You can move around in many ways, including using the arrow keys, the mouse, and special keys (such as PgUp and PgDn). You are not restricted to one method of moving around in a document; people who use a mouse often use keyboard shortcuts as well.

Note: *You can move the insertion point anywhere within the document's text. You cannot, however, move the insertion point beyond the end mark.*

The I-beam serves a special function: it moves the insertion point to a new location on-screen. Suppose that you have just finished typing a three-paragraph letter and you want to edit a word in the first paragraph.

Use the mouse to position the I-beam to the right of the word, and then click the mouse button. The insertion point moves to the I-beam's position. Remember that the I-beam is different from the insertion point. You use the I-beam to move the insertion point (or to select text, as you learn later in this lesson); the insertion point is where your editing takes place.

You can also use the mouse to scroll the screen with the usual Windows methods:

- To scroll up (toward the beginning of the document), click the up arrow at the top of the scroll bar.

- To scroll down, click the down arrow at the bottom of the scroll bar.

- To scroll left or right, click the left or right arrow at either end of the horizontal scroll bar.

- Click and hold down the scroll arrows to scroll continuously.

- Drag the scroll box—which represents your position in the document—in either direction.

- Click in the shaded area on either side of the scroll box to move the scroll box in that direction one screen at a time.

Scrolling isn't quite the same as moving. When you scroll, you display a different part of the document, but the insertion point remains where it was. You often will use the scroll bars together with the I-beam—first scrolling to display the text where you want to move, and then clicking the I-beam to move the insertion point to that location.

Finding and Replacing Text

In a long document, finding a single word may be difficult. And if your document contains many occurrences of a word or phrase that you must change, making the changes one by one can be tedious. Write can help you with both tasks through the **F**ind and **R**eplace commands in the Fi**n**d menu.

When you ask Write to find text, the program searches through the document from the insertion point forward, selecting the first occurrence of the text. When the end of the document is reached, Write starts at the top of the document and searches down from there.

10

When you need to change a word or phrase, you can have Write locate the text for you and wait for your response. You can skip that occurrence and search for the next one, or make the replacement and then search for the next occurrence.

Use the Replace dialog box to search for and replace words or phrases in a document.

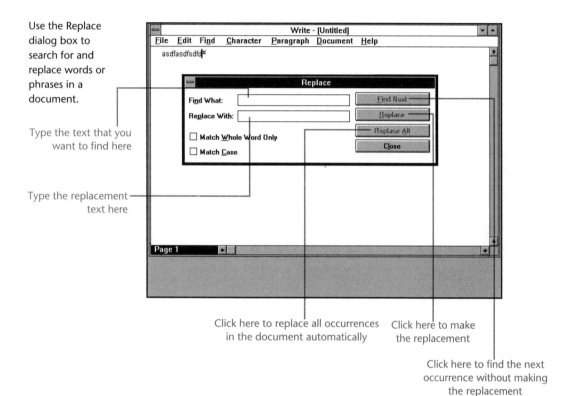

Type the text that you want to find here

Type the replacement text here

Click here to replace all occurrences in the document automatically

Click here to make the replacement

Click here to find the next occurrence without making the replacement

Selecting and Editing Text

With Write, you can easily edit or revise your documents. Editing includes such changes as inserting and deleting text and selecting and deselecting sections of the document for enhancement (see the next section for details on enhancing the text).

The simplest way to edit text is to delete and insert characters. Start by moving the insertion point to the location at which you want to delete or insert text. Press the Backspace key to erase the character to the left of the insertion point, or press the Del (Delete) key to erase the character to the right of the insertion point. If you hold down the key, you erase a whole string of characters. Then type the new text. As you type, the new text is inserted to the left of the insertion point, and the text to the right moves farther right (and down, if necessary) to make room for the new text.

Windows programs generally follow the same methodology: select, then do. For example, to copy a file in File Manager, you select the file and then execute the **F**ile **C**opy command. In a word processing program such as Write, more complicated editing requires that you begin by selecting the text you want to edit. To *select* simply means to highlight text, identifying it as the text you want to affect when you press a key or choose an editing command.

Selected text is highlighted, ready to be edited.

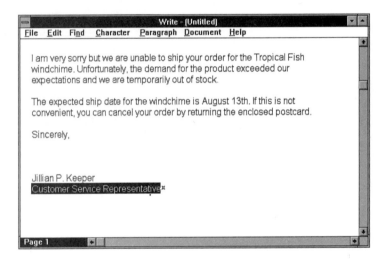

Follow these steps to select text with the mouse:

1. Move the I-beam to one side of the text you want to select.

2. Hold down the left mouse button.

3. Drag the I-beam over the text you want to select (you can drag in any direction).

4. Release the mouse button.

If you have problems... If you need to select more than one full screen of text, continue holding down the mouse button while you drag the I-beam to the bottom of the screen. The screen scrolls automatically when the I-beam touches the bottom of the screen.

Note: *Alternatively, you can double-click a word to select it. You can use Ctrl+click in a sentence to select the sentence, and double-click in a paragraph to select the whole paragraph. To select a line, you can position the mouse in the selection area (when the mouse is in the left margin, the pointer changes to a left-pointing pointer).*

When you finish editing the selected text, you may want to deselect it. Position the I-beam anywhere in your document and click the left mouse button to deselect the current selection.

Enhancing and Formatting Text

Enhanced text not only makes a document look better by adding variety to your pages, but also helps make the document more organized and thus more readable, by adding emphasis to important words or headings. Write includes many tools for enhancing characters, including bold and italic, various font styles, and many font sizes. All the text-enhancement commands are located in the **C**haracter menu.

A check mark indicates each currently selected text-enhancement command in the **C**haracter menu.

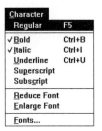

To enhance existing text, you must first select the text, as described in the preceding section. You can also enhance text by first choosing the enhancement to turn it on, then typing the text, and finally choosing the enhancement a second time to turn it off.

Consider using the Find feature to locate key phrases you want to enhance. See the section "Finding and Replacing Text" earlier in this lesson.

Write provides three levels of formatting: character, paragraph, and document. See the section "Task: Emphasize Characters" next in this lesson for information on character formatting. See the section "Task: Align Paragraphs" for information on paragraph formatting. Document formatting is covered later in this lesson in the section "Task: Change the Margins."

Task: Emphasize Characters

Bold text stands out and is excellent for adding emphasis to headlines, subheadings, or other important text. Italic text adds more subtle emphasis and is useful for identifying titles and names within a document. Underlining, a holdover from the days of the typewriter, is less useful but may be appropriate for headings in tables or for dividing sections of text. Superscript and subscript characters are raised or lowered, respectively, from the rest of the text and are used for footnotes and scientific notations. The Regular command on the Character menu removes these enhancements and returns the selected text to its normal appearance.

Follow these steps to enhance text in the sample letter:

1. Select the phrase "Tropical Fish windchime."

2. Pull down the Character menu and choose Italic.

4. Select the phrase "August 13th."

5. Pull down the Character menu and choose Bold.

The sample letter
with italicized and
bold text.

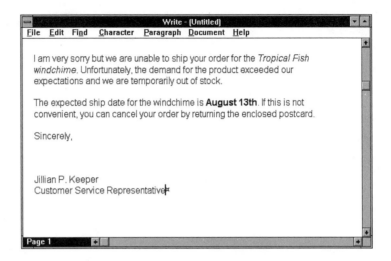

Task: Reduce and Enlarge Characters

A quick way to make text larger or smaller is to use the commands in the **C**haracter menu. Each time you choose the **R**educe Font or **E**nlarge Font command, the text changes to the next smaller or larger font size (see the next section for more details on fonts). Typically, standard font sizes are 10, 12, 14, 18, 24, and 36 point. If you select 10-point type and choose the **E**nlarge Font command, for example, the text enlarges to 12 points, rather than 11.

To reduce and enlarge characters in the sample letter, follow these steps:

1. Select the date at the top of the letter.

2. Pull down the **C**haracter menu and choose **E**nlarge Font.

The date is now
larger than the rest
of the text.

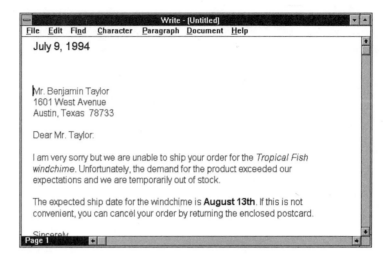

3. Select the phrase "Customer Service Representative."

4. Pull down the **C**haracter menu and choose **R**educe Font.

The signature title is
now smaller than
the rest of the text.

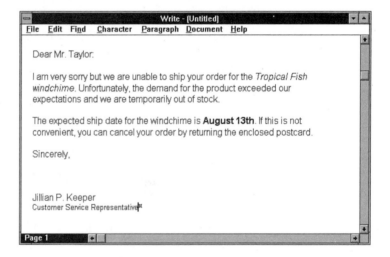

You can also use the Font dialog box to change the size of characters, as explained in the following section.

If you have problems...	If you don't like the enhancement you have chosen, select the text, pull down the **C**haracter menu, and choose Re**g**ular. You can also use the **U**ndo command on the **E**dit menu, provided you have not taken any other action on the document after making the enhancement. The **U**ndo command reverses only the *last* action taken on the document.

Task: Change the Font

Typeface
The design of a set of type, differentiated from others by weight, posture, and size.

A font is a style of type, or a *typeface*, in a particular size or range of sizes. Write enables you to change your text to any font you have available in your computer or printer. Font sizes are measured in *points*, where 72 points equal one inch. Newspaper text may be 9 or 10 points in size, and headlines may be 18 to 36 points.

Point
A unit of measurement used for fonts. Select a higher point size for a larger font.

Windows supplies two types of fonts that you can use immediately. Three fonts—Modern, Roman, and Script—are included. These fonts are Windows system fonts and are rarely used because the second type of font used with Windows, the TrueType fonts, produces better quality results. TrueType fonts look crisp on-screen and print with high quality on any printer that Windows supports. Other fonts may also be available for you to use. (To learn more about fonts, see Lesson 6, "Controlling Printers and Fonts.")

Use the **F**onts command on the **C**haracter menu to display the Font dialog box, in which you can change not only the font but also the font size and style. The fonts, styles, and sizes that appear in the Font dialog box depend on the fonts you have available on your computer or in your printer.

To change the fonts for the sample letter, follow these steps:

1. Select the entire text of the letter.

2. Pull down the **C**haracter menu and choose **F**onts.

The Font dialog box appears.

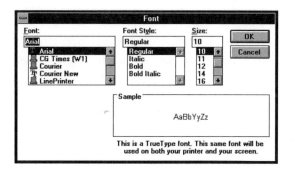

3. Click the Times New Roman font (scroll the list, if necessary).

An icon to the left of each font indicates the font type. A TT icon indicates a TrueType font, and a printer icon indicates a printer font. No icon indicates a system font.

Notice the Font St**y**le list, where you can select the font style you want. Notice also the **S**ize list box, where you can select the point size you want, or type the size you want in the **S**ize box. If you don't specify a size, Write matches the current font sizes in the document.

Note: *The Sample box in the Font dialog box shows you how the font will look in your document.*

4. Choose OK.

The font change for the letter is immediately reflected on-screen. Notice that the Times New Roman font is narrower than the Arial font, and the text has been reformatted to reflect that change.

Task: Align Paragraphs

Paragraph-level formatting applies to entire paragraphs—remember that a paragraph is any block of text that ends when you press the Enter key. You can align paragraphs of text at the left margin, the right margin, or both margins (justified); or you can center paragraphs between margins. Centered text is centered between the left and right margins. Justified text is aligned at both the left and right margins, so the text stretches from margin to margin.

Note: *By default, Write's paragraphs are aligned at the left, but you can easily change the alignment for any paragraph you select.*

To center text in the sample letter, follow these steps:

1. Select the date at the top of the letter.

2. Pull down the **P**aragraph menu.

A check mark in the **P**aragraph menu indicates the current paragraph alignment.

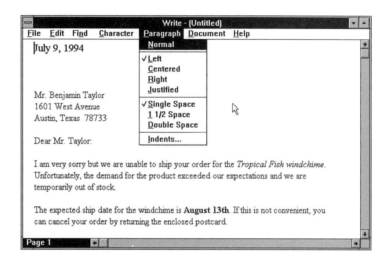

3. Choose **C**entered.

4. Select the date again.

5. Pull down the **P**aragraph menu and choose **R**ight to align the date at the right margin.

If you change your mind, you can return the text alignment to the left margin.

6. Select the date again.

7. Pull down the **P**aragraph menu and choose **L**eft.

Task: Change the Margins

Document-level formatting applies to the entire document. You can create headers and footers, set up custom tabs, change the margins, and add page numbers. These features are available through the **D**ocument menu. You use the **P**age Layout option to access the Page Layout dialog box, which has options to change the left, right, top, and bottom margins, as well as to add page numbers to the document. By default, the left and right margins are set to 1.25 inches, with the top and bottom margins set to 1 inch.

Follow these steps to change the margins for the letter to 1 inch on all sides:

1. Pull down the **D**ocument menu and choose **P**age Layout. The Page Layout dialog box appears.

2. Double-click the **L**eft Margin text box to select the current setting of 1.25 inches.

3. Type **1**. Note that you do not have to type the inches (") mark.

4. Double-click the **R**ight Margin text box to select the current setting of 1.25 inches.

5. Type **1**.

6. Click OK to change the left and right margins to 1 inch.

Saving and Opening Files

Until you save a document, it's like a song on the radio. If the radio goes off, you lose the song. A saved file, however, is like a song on a cassette tape. Even if the electricity goes off, you still have the song because it was recorded on the tape. Saving the document "records" it on disk. After you save a document, you can open it at a later time to edit or print it.

Task: Save a Document

Before you save a document, it has no name; it is called Untitled. The first time you save the document, you give it a name, which appears in the title bar at the top of the Write window. Your file name can contain up to eight letters or numbers; Write automatically assigns the three-letter extension WRI to each file name. Refer to the section "Understanding File Names" in Lesson 8 for a discussion of the characters that can be used in file names.

Note: *You should always save your document before you print it.*

To save and name the sample letter, follow these steps:

1. Pull down the **F**ile menu and choose **S**ave.

2. In the File **N**ame text box, type **taylor**.

The Save As dialog box appears automatically because the file has not been previously saved.

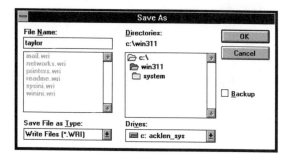

10

3. Choose OK.

Notice the **B**ackup check box. If you check this box, the previously saved version of TAYLOR.WRI will be renamed TAYLOR.BKP, and the current version on-screen will be saved to TAYLOR.WRI. If you do not check this box, the previous version will be overwritten by the newer one when you save the file.

Note: *When you save a document, you save it as a computer file.*

Now that the document has a file name, you have two options the next time you want to save the file. If you want to keep only one copy of the file on disk, pull down the **F**ile menu and choose **S**ave. This command saves the new version of the file on top of the previous version, thus replacing it. You can use **S**ave only if the document has been previously saved.

The second option is to choose the Save **A**s command and give the file a new name. By creating a new file, you preserve the previous version of the file. This approach is helpful if you want to keep track of revisions to a certain document, or if you are working with forms and want to save the completed form under a different name (so you preserve the original form file).

Task: Open an Existing File

After a file has been saved, you can open it later to edit or print it. The **O**pen command in the **F**ile menu displays a list of files and directories on the drive. When you open an existing file, the one you're currently working on closes. If you have made changes to the current document since you last saved it, Write asks whether you want to save your changes.

To retrieve an existing file, follow these steps:

1. From the **F**ile menu, choose the **O**pen command.

The Open dialog box displays a list of files and directories on the current drive.

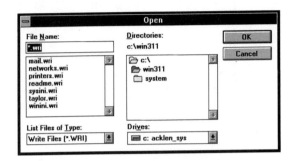

2. In the Dri**v**es list, select the drive containing the file you want to open, if the drive is different from the current drive.

3. If necessary, select the Windows directory in the **D**irectories list. The current directory is shown above the **D**irectories list.

5. In the File **N**ame list, click the README.WRI file. Or, in the File **N**ame text box, type the name of the file you want to open.

6. Choose OK.

Task: Print a Document

When you print a document, Write uses the default printer settings. These settings are specified during installation and can be changed through the Printer program in Control Panel or through Write. If it isn't necessary to change the defaults, all you have to do is print. However, if you find it necessary to make changes, you can make them before you print.

Note: *You can print other documents in addition to those you create in Write. You can print a README file or any other text file, such as a document created in Word for DOS.*

To change print settings and print a document, follow these steps:

1. Pull down the **F**ile menu and choose **P**rint.

By default, the Print dialog box is configured to print the entire document.

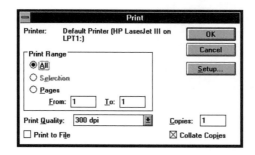

2. Verify the correct Print Range option. The **A**ll option is selected by default. You can also choose to print selected text or a range of consecutive pages.

3. If necessary, type in the **C**opies box the number of copies you want to print.

4. If you need to select a printer, choose **S**etup.

The Print Setup dialog box appears.

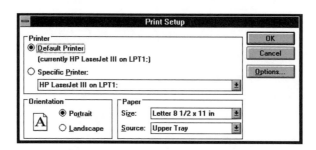

5. To change to a different printer, select the printer you want from the Printer group. You can select either the **D**efault Printer or another printer from the Specific **P**rinter list, which lists all the printers installed in Windows.

6. Choose OK to close the Print Setup dialog box and return to the Print dialog box.

7. Choose OK to print your document.

Task: Exit Write

After you create, save, and print your document, you probably are ready to call it a day (and with a little luck, it's quitting time too). This task is the easiest part of all.

To quit Write, follow these simple steps:

1. Pull down the **F**ile menu and choose E**x**it.

If you have made changes to your document since you last saved it, Write prompts you to save them.

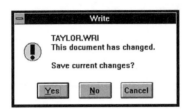

2. If necessary, save the document.

Summary

To	Do This
Start the Write program	Open the Accessories group window. Double-click the Write icon.
Type text on the screen	Press the keys on the keyboard. The characters you type will appear to the left of the insertion point.
Move around in a document	Press the arrow keys, PgUp, PgDn, Home, and End; or use the mouse to move the I-beam to a new location.
Find and replace text	Use the **F**ind and **R**eplace commands on the Fi**n**d menu. In the Replace dialog box, make the appropriate selections to replace a word or phrase.
Insert text	Move the insertion point to the place where you want the text inserted. Type the text.
Delete text	Press the Backspace key to erase text to the left of the insertion point; press the Del key to erase text to the right of the insertion point.

10

To	Do This
Select text	Move the I-beam to the beginning of the text you want to select. Hold down the left mouse button while you drag the I-beam across the text. Release the mouse button.
Deselect text	Position the I-beam anywhere in the document and click the mouse button.
Bold text	Select the text. Pull down the **C**haracter menu and choose **B**old.
Italicize text	Select the text. Pull down the **C**haracter menu and choose **I**talic.
Underline text	Select the text. Pull down the **C**haracter menu and choose **U**nderline.
Superscript text	Select the text. Pull down the **C**haracter menu and choose Su**p**erscript.
Subscript text	Select the text. Pull down the **C**haracter menu and choose Sub**s**cript.
Reduce characters	Select the text. Pull down the **C**haracter menu and choose **R**educe Font.
Enlarge characters	Select the text. Pull down the **C**haracter menu and choose **E**nlarge Font.
Change the font	If necessary, select the text. Pull down the **C**haracter menu and choose **F**onts. Select a font from the **F**ont list. If necessary, choose a style from the Font St**y**le list. If necessary, choose a size from the **S**ize list or type a size in the **S**ize box.
Align text	Select the text. Pull down the **P**aragraph menu and choose the alignment you want (left, right, centered, or justified).
Change the margins	Pull down the **D**ocument menu and choose **P**age Layout. Double-click the text boxes for the margin settings you want to change. Type the new settings. Click OK.
Save a document	Pull down the **F**ile menu and choose **S**ave. If necessary, type a file name in the File **N**ame text box. Choose OK.
Open an existing document	Pull down the **F**ile menu and choose **O**pen. Select the drive and directory containing the file you want to open. Click the file and choose OK. If you have made changes to the current document, you will be prompted to save them before Write will open another document.

(continues)

To	Do This
Print a document	Pull down the **F**ile menu and choose **P**rint. Make any necessary changes. If you need to select another printer, choose **S**etup. Choose OK.

On Your Own
Estimated time: 15 minutes

1. Start the Write program and create a short memo.

2. Center the heading MEMORANDUM at the top of the page.

3. Bold the memo headings (To:, From:, Subject:, and Date:).

4. Enlarge the characters on the memo headings.

5. Change the font for the text of the memo.

6. Type this paragraph explaining your vacation plans for the next week:

    I will be out of the office on vacation for the next two weeks beginning on Monday. My assistant, Heather West, will be handling my accounts while I am gone. Please contact her if you have any questions.

7. Revise the paragraph to indicate that you will be on vacation for the next three weeks.

8. Print the memo.

9. Save the memo under the file name VACATION.WRI.

Lesson 11

Using Mail and PC Fax

 Windows for Workgroups includes an electronic mail program that allows you to communicate with other users on your network. The Mail program enables you and others in your workgroup to send and receive messages. In addition, you can attach a file, such as a word processing document or a spreadsheet, to a message. Finally, you can manage your incoming and outgoing messages by creating folders in which to store the messages.

Windows for Workgroups 3.11 introduces a new program: PC Fax. PC Fax enables you to send and receive faxes in Windows. You can send a fax from within a Windows document or from within Mail. Faxes that you receive show up as Mail messages in your mailbox, even if you are not on a network.

This lesson teaches you how to

- Start Mail and connect to a post office
- Send a message
- Read, reply to, forward, and delete messages
- Attach a file to a message
- Create a message folder and save messages in it
- Send a fax from an application or mail
- Receive, view, and print faxes

Using Electronic Mail

Electronic mail systems, also called E-mail, enable users to exchange messages across a network. Files (such as documents or spreadsheets) can be attached to messages and sent to other users for review. The attached file becomes a user's personal copy that can be modified without affecting the original copy.

Post office

A workstation computer that collects and disperses mail messages for each mail user on the network.

The mail system is maintained by one workgroup computer, called a *post office*, which keeps a list of all the system users. Mail messages are stored in directories for each mail system user on the post office computer. A post office computer is also known as a mail server.

The Windows for Workgroups Schedule+ and Microsoft at Work PC Fax programs use the post office to coordinate with other users on the network. For example, you can send a fax from Mail or from an application, and Schedule+ uses the mail server to let you view free times and busy times of others in your workgroup so that you can schedule meetings.

Task: Start the Mail Program

The first time you sign in to mail, you need to connect to an existing post office. You may have to set up your own user account, although in most cases, a system administrator will do this for you when the post office is set up. If you are in charge of setting up these options for your workgroup, consult Que's *Using Windows*, 3.11 Edition, Special Edition, for a complete discussion on setting up a post office and creating user accounts.

To start Mail and connect to a post office, follow these steps:

1. Double-click the Network group icon in Program Manager.

The Mail icon looks like a brass mail slot with envelopes in it.

2. Double-click the Mail icon.

The first time you execute this step, Mail displays the Welcome to Mail dialog box.

Windows for Workgroups greets new users and invites them to connect to an existing post office.

3. Click the **C**onnect to an Existing Postoffice option and then click OK.

You use the Network Disk Resources dialog box to connect to an existing post office.

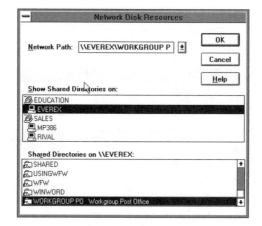

4. If you know the location of your workgroup's post office, type the path in the **N**etwork Path text box. Use the format *computername**sharename*. (The term *computername* refers to the name of the computer and the drive on that computer where the Windows for Workgroups software is installed. The term *sharename* refers to the directory in *computername* that contains your workgroup's post office.)

If you are unsure of the path of the post office, check with your system administrator.

5. Click OK.

6. If the post office directory is password-protected, Mail displays the Enter Shared Directory Password dialog box. Type the password in the text box (the characters appear as asterisks) and then click OK.

Mail displays a dialog box that asks whether you have an account.

7. Choose **Y**es if your system administrator has created an account for you.

8. You are prompted for a password to gain access to your mailbox. Unless the system administrator specified a specific password, the default password is PASSWORD. You should immediately change the default password to one of your own to protect the privacy of your mail.

The Mail application window and Inbox window at startup.

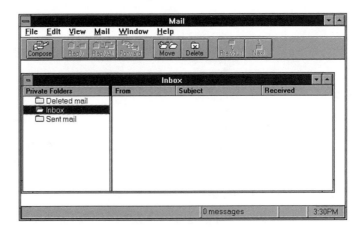

If you have problems...	Before any workgroup member can begin to send and receive mail, the member must set up a user account with the post office. Check with your system administrator.

After your post office and user account are established, all you have to do is start Mail and type your password to access your mail. This sign-in process prevents other users from reading your mail or sending mail messages in your name. To preserve the security, immediately change the default password and do not give your password to other users.

To sign in to Mail, follow these steps:

1. Double-click the Network icon in Program Manager.

2. Double-click the Mail icon.

3. Enter your password in the **P**assword text box.

4. Choose OK to continue.

11

You are prompted for a password when you sign in to Mail.

Note: *If you don't need sign-in security, select the Remember Password check box in the Mail Sign In dialog box. Thereafter, Mail will not prompt you for your password.*

Task: Send a Message

A mail message can be sent to a single user or a group of users on your network, depending on how you address the message. The Mail program supports the carbon copy function, enabling you to send copies of the message to users other than the recipients. You can also set a return re-ceipt option that sends a confirmation back to you when your message has been received.

Follow these steps to send a message:

1. Start the Mail program and type your password.

2. Click the Compose button.

You use the Send Note dialog box to send messages to other users on your network.

Click here to send
the message

Click here to type
the message text

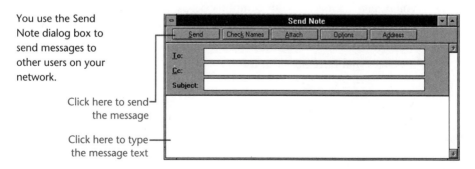

3. In the **T**o text box, type the user name of the recipient. To include multiple names, type a semicolon and a space between the names.

   Note: *You can type the first few characters of a user name and have Mail supply the rest of the name by pressing Alt+K. You must enter enough characters to allow Mail to determine that the user name is unique. Using fewer characters causes the Check Name dialog box to be displayed.*

4. To send a carbon copy of the message to another person, type the user name in the **C**c text box. To include multiple names, type a semicolon and a space between the names.

5. Type the subject of the message in the Subject text box. You don't have to type a subject, but a subject listing helps workgroup members sort and prioritize incoming mail.

6. Click in the message area to move the cursor down to the message window; then type your message.

7. Click the **S**end button to send the message.

Task: Read a Message

All your incoming messages are stored in the Inbox folder, which is created automatically when your mailbox is set up. After you read your messages, you can reply to them, forward them to other users, store them in a different folder, print them, or delete them.

Mail can notify you of incoming messages in several ways. If you are working in another application, your computer can beep at you. You can reduce Mail to an icon on your desktop and, when you receive a message, the computer beeps, and the icon changes to show an envelope popping out of the mail slot. Finally, if you are viewing the Inbox folder when you receive a message, your computer beeps, the mouse pointer briefly changes to an envelope icon, and the new message appears in the list of messages in the Inbox folder. A closed envelope icon appears next to messages that have not been read.

Follow these steps to read a message:

1. Start the Mail program and type your password.

2. If necessary, open the Inbox folder.

Closed envelope icon indicates a new message

The Inbox window displays information about each message.

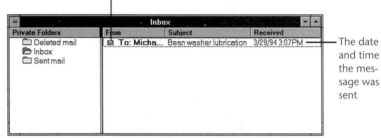

The date and time the message was sent

3. Double-click the message you want to read.

Note: *If a message has a file attached to it, an icon appears in the text area of the message window. Double-click the icon to open the attached file with its associated application.*

Task: Reply to a Message

When you reply to a message, the message is automatically addressed to the sender for you. The original message is included as a part of the reply. You can add your comments on top of the original message, or you can delete the original message.

To reply to a message, follow these steps:

1. Start the Mail program and type your password.

2. In the Inbox window, double-click the message you want to reply to.

3. Click the Reply button.

The Mail system automatically addresses the reply message and includes the original subject and message text.

Click here to send your response

The original subject appears here

Type your response here

The name of the original sender

The original message text appears here

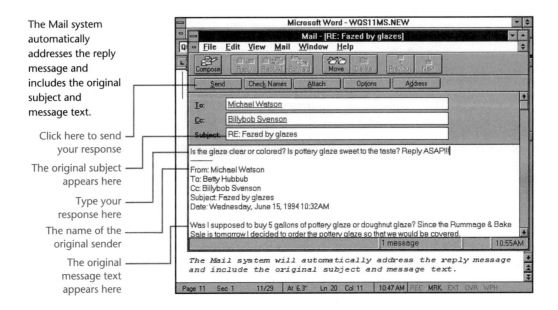

4. Type your response to the message.

5. If you prefer, you can delete the original message text from the reply message.

6. Click the **S**end button to send your response.

Task: Forward a Message

In this information-driven age, the capability to pass information to others quickly is a great advantage. Because your workgroup may depend on shared information, you can easily forward a message to any other user on your network.

The steps for forwarding a message are almost identical to replying to a message. The only difference is that you have to address a forwarded message.

To forward a mail message, follow these steps:

1. Start the Mail program and type your password.

2. In the Inbox window, double-click the message you want to forward.

3. Click the Forward button.

Mail displays the
message in a Send
Note window, and
FW appears at the
beginning of the
Subject text box.

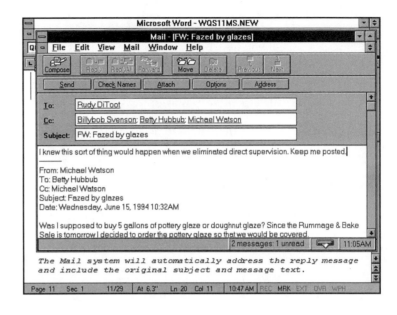

4. Change the addresses, change the subject, or modify the text as necessary.

5. Click the **S**end button. Mail sends the message.

Task: Print a Message

The purpose of electronic mail is to cut down on the amount of paper passed back and forth. At times, however, you will need to print a copy of your message.

To print a message, follow these steps:

1. Start the Mail program and type your password.

2. In the Inbox window, click the message you want to print.

3. Pull down the **F**ile menu and choose **P**rint.

   Note: *Mail can print more than one message at a time. Use Ctrl+click or Shift+click to select multiple messages before you choose **File P**rint.*

Task: Delete a Message

If you have no reason to save a message, you should delete it to conserve disk space and reduce the clutter in your Mail folders. You can move files to the Deleted Mail folder at any time. When you quit Mail, the program deletes those messages.

Follow these steps to delete a Mail message:

1. Start the Mail program and type your password.

2. In the Inbox window, click the message you want to delete.

3. Click the Delete button. The message is moved to the Deleted Mail folder.

   Note: *Alternatively, you can press the Del key or drag the message to the Deleted Mail folder to delete it.*

If you have problems...	If you mistakenly delete a message, you can open the Deleted Mail folder and drag the message back to its former folder or to any other folder, as long as you have not exited the Mail program. If you delete messages from the Deleted Mai! folder, they are deleted from the disk and cannot be retrieved. When you exit Mail, the program deletes the messages in the Deleted Mail folder; at that point, you cannot retrieve them.

Task: Attach a File to a Message

Mail allows you to attach a file to a message, so that the recipient of the message receives an actual copy of the file along with the message. For example, if you want to distribute to several coworkers a copy of a document you have been working on, you can address a message to those coworkers, explaining what the document is about, and attach the document file to the message. Each addressee will receive the message and a copy of the file. Think how much quicker and easier this method is than hand-delivering the file on floppy disks!

Follow these steps to attach a file to a mail message:

1. Start the Mail program and type your password.

2. Click the Compose button to create a new message.

3. While composing the message text in the Send Note window, position the cursor at the point in the text where you want the attachment to appear.

4. Click the **A**ttach button. The Attach dialog box appears.

In the Attach dialog box, you can select a file to attach to a message.

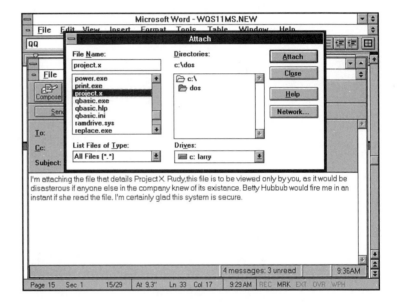

5. Using the directory and file lists to locate the file, click the file you want to attach to your message.

6. Click **A**ttach.

The Attach dialog box remains on-screen, and an icon corresponding to the type of file you selected (for example, the Paintbrush icon for BMP files, a notebook icon for TXT files, or the WinWord icon for Word DOC files) appears at the insertion point in the text.

This Send note
window shows an
unsent message
with a file attached.

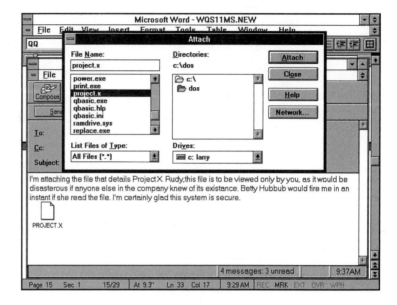

7. Repeat steps 3 and 4 for as many files as you need to attach. Then click the Close button in the Attach File dialog box.

8. When you finish composing the message, click the **S**end button to send it as you would any other message.

When receiving your message, the recipient will see the icons representing the attached file embedded in the message text. The recipient can view the attached file by double-clicking the icon, which launches the originating application and opens the file. If the recipient does not have the correct application that will open the file, an error box indicates that the file has no association.

Task: Create a New Folder

A folder system can help you organize your mail messages. You can create and maintain a folder system similar to the filing system for your paper documents.

When you open your account, Mail provides three folders: Deleted Mail, Inbox, and Sent Mail. The Inbox and Sent Mail folders may become cluttered because Mail brings every message you receive into the Inbox folder, and Mail stores a copy of every message you send in the Sent Mail folder. You can add folders to handle this overflow. The folders can be private folders for your exclusive use or shared folders.

Mail displays folders as yellow folder icons, with names, on the left side of the Mail window. To add a folder, follow these steps:

1. Start the Mail program and type your password.

2. Pull down the **F**ile menu and choose New **F**older.

The New Folder
dialog box appears.

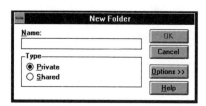

3. In the **N**ame text box, type a name for the folder. (You can use any combination of characters, including spaces.) For efficiency, you may want to keep the names of your folders brief.

4. In the Type section, click the **P**rivate or **S**hared option.

Private messages stored in a private folder can be viewed only by you.

Shared messages stored in a shared folder are accessible to other users in your post office. To set other users' access to a shared folder, click the **O**ptions button in the New Folder dialog box, and then select or deselect the **R**ead, **W**rite, and **D**elete options in the Other Users Can group.

5. Click OK. An icon of a folder appears next to the name of the folder in the Mail window. Folders are listed alphabetically by name.

Note: *A folder is visible only when its folder type is selected. Click on the heading of the Folders window to toggle between Private Folders and Shared Folders.*

Task: Save a Message to a Folder

You can save messages to a private folder accessible only to you, or to a shared folder accessible to others on your network.

To save a message to a folder, follow these steps:

1. Start the Mail program and type your password.

2. Click the message you want to save to a folder.

3. To copy the message, open the **F**ile menu and choose **C**opy. The Copy Message dialog box appears.

To move the message, click the Move button in the toolbar. The Move Message dialog box appears.

The Copy Message and Move Message dialog boxes are identical except for their names and functions.

4. Click a folder in the Copy **T**o or Move **T**o list box.

As in any list, you can scroll the list to find a name that does not appear in the box. You cannot scroll horizontally to see beyond the right side of the box.

5. Click OK.

Mail copies or moves the message to the new folder and displays your Inbox window. When you select the folder to which the message was moved or copied, the listing of the message appears, with a gray envelope and a note icon next to it.

Using PC Fax

Windows for Workgroups 3.11 includes PC Fax, which allows you to send a fax from within Windows applications or from Mail. In the Mail program, the mail message is the fax document. In an application, the active document is the fax document.

When you install PC Fax, a new Fa**x** menu appears in the Mail menu bar. Some Windows applications, such as Microsoft Excel and Word for Windows, automatically display a Sen**d** command in the **F**ile menu. This command makes faxing a document as easy as printing.

Task: Send a Fax

Applications that are designed to work with Microsoft Mail (a **Send** command appears on the **F**ile menu) can send a fax directly from the application. Applications that are not Mail-enabled can send a fax if you select the fax/modem as the printer and then print the document to the fax/modem.

To send a fax of a document, such as a Word for Windows document, follow these steps:

1. Start the Mail program and type your password.

2. Start the application and then open the document you want to send.

3. Pull down the **F**ile menu and choose Sen**d**. The Send Note dialog box appears. Alternatively, if you set up the fax/modem as a printer, open the **F**ile menu and choose **P**rint; then click OK.

You enter the telephone number and a message to accompany your fax.

WQS11M .NEW
Edit **Help**

| Send | Check Names | Attach | Options | Address | Cancel |

To: [FAX: BugSpit@5814663]

Cc:

Subject: WQS11M_.NEW

WQS11M_.NEW

4. Type the name and phone number in the **T**o and **C**c text boxes, using one of the following examples:

[fax: *name @ phonenumber*]

[fax: *phonenumber*]

If you do not want to send the fax to a specific name, use the example that shows just a phone number. Make sure that you enclose the entry in square brackets and follow the word *fax* with a colon.

The preceding figure shows a fax that is being sent from within Word 2 for Windows. Notice the attached text document icon. This icon will print as a text document when it is received by a fax machine.

5. Click the **S**end button.

In Mail, the only difference between a Mail message and a fax is the address. You can attach one or more documents, such as a spreadsheet file.

Follow these steps to send a fax from Mail:

1. Start the Mail program and type your password.

2. Click the Compose button.

3. Type the name and phone number in the **T**o amd **C**c text boxes, using one of the following examples:

    [fax: *name @ phonenumber*]

    [fax: *phonenumber*]

    If you do not want to send the fax to a specific name, use the example that shows just a phone number. Make sure that you enclose the entry in square brackets and follow the word *fax* with a colon.

4. Type the subject and any message text.

5. If you want to attach a document, click the **A**ttach button. The Attach dialog box appears, where you can select the document. Click **A**ttach. If necessary, select additional documents. Click Cl**o**se when you are finished.

6. Click the **S**end button.

If you have problems...

If you enter an incorrect name in the **T**o or **C**c box, a Mail alert box warns you that names could not be matched against the address list. This message means that the names and phone numbers were invalid or that the structure of the entries was incorrect. In this case, make sure that you correctly typed names that were in the post office address list, correctly typed phone numbers, enclosed the entry line in square brackets, and followed the word *fax* with a colon.

Task: Receive and View a Fax

A fax machine receives a fax sent from PC Fax in the same way it receives a fax sent from another fax machine. If you have PC Fax set up to accept incoming faxes, each new fax that PC Fax receives is treated like a new Mail message.

11

The new fax appears as an item in the Mail Inbox.

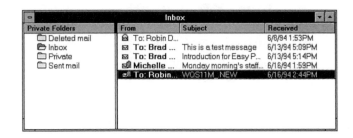

Follow these steps to read a fax:

1. Start the Mail program and type your password.

2. Open the Inbox folder and double-click the fax.

3. View the fax, or double-click any icon to view the fax as an embedded document.

If you have problems...

If your Mail program does not have the Fa**x** menu name on the menu bar, you need to configure the fax/modem in the Fax program in Control Panel. Double-click the Fax icon in Control Panel. If you have set up Mail and have connected to a post office, the Fax Modem box appears. Otherwise, the Microsoft at Work PC Fax dialog box appears. Click E-Mail and Fax or Fax Only, depending on whether you plan to use the Mail program to send messages to other users. If you click Fax Only, you will be prompted to set up Mail after you configure the fax/modem.

Click the **A**dd button in the Fax Modems dialog box. In the Add Fax Modems dialog box, click the type of modem you want to add; then click OK. In the Fax Phone Number dialog box, type all the components of your fax number and click OK. In the Fax Modems dialog box, click **S**etup and set the options you prefer. Click OK.

A fax can contain an attached document. If you receive this document as a Mail message with an attached document, and you have a copy of the application that created the document, you can open and edit the attached document by double-clicking the document's icon. The application will start and open the document, which you then can edit or save.

Task: Print a Fax

You can print a fax from Mail. When you print a fax, the attached files will not be printed. These attachments must be printed from the application in which they were created.

Follow these steps to print a fax from Mail:

1. Start the Mail program and type your password.

2. In the Inbox folder, click the fax you want to print.

3. Pull down the **F**ile menu and choose **P**rint.

4. Click OK.

Follow these steps to print an attachment:

1. Start the Mail program and type your password.

2. Double-click the fax that contains the attachment you want to print.

3. Double-click the icon that represents the attached file. This starts the application and opens the file.

4. Pull down the **F**ile menu and choose **P**rint.

5. Click OK.

Summary

To	Do This
Start the Mail program and connect to a post office	Double-click the Network group icon in Program Manager. Double-click the Mail program icon. Click the Connect to an Existing Postoffice option and then click OK. Type the path of the existing post office in the **N**etwork Path text box. Click OK. Type the password for the post office in the text box and then click OK. Choose **Y**es to indicate

11

To	Do This
	that the system administrator has set up an account for you. To sign in to Mail, type the password for your mailbox.
Sign in to Mail	Double-click the Network group icon in Program Manager. Double-click the Mail program icon. Type your password and then click OK.
Send a message	Click the Compose button. Type the user name(s) of the recipient(s) in the **T**o text box. If necessary, type the user name(s) in the **C**c text box. Type a subject in the Sub**j**ect text box. Click in the message area and type your message. Click the **S**end button.
Read a message	If necessary, open the Inbox folder. Double-click the message you want to read.
Reply to a message	Double-click the message you want to reply to. Click the Reply button. Type your response and click the **S**end button.
Forward a message	Double-click the message you want to forward. Click the Forward button. Change the addresses, change the subject, or modify the text as necessary. Click the **S**end button.
Print a message	Click the message you want to print. Pull down the **F**ile menu and choose **P**rint.
Delete a message	Click the message you want to delete. Click the Delete button.
Attach a file to a message	Click the Compose button. While composing the message text, position the cursor where you want the attachment to appear. Click the **A**ttach button. Click the file you want to attach, and then click **A**ttach. When you are finished composing the message, click the **S**end button to send the message.
Create a new folder	Pull down the **F**ile menu and choose New **F**older. Type the name for the folder in the **N**ame text box. Click the **P**rivate or **S**hared option. Click OK.
Save a message to a folder	Click the message you want to save to a folder. To copy the message, open the **F**ile menu and choose **C**opy. The Copy Message dialog box appears. To move the message, click the Move button in the toolbar. The Move Message dialog box appears. Click a folder in the Move **T**o or Copy **T**o list box. Click OK.

(continues)

To	Do This
Send a fax from an application	Start the application and open or create the document. Pull down the **F**ile menu and choose Sen**d**. If no Sen**d** option is present, choose **P**rint and then click OK. Type the name and phone number in the **T**o text box. If necessary, do the same for the **C**c text box. Click the **S**end button.
Send a fax from Mail program	Click the Compose button. Type the name and phone number in the **T**o text box. If necessary, do the same for the **C**c text box. Type the subject and the message text. If you want to send an attachment, click the **A**ttach button. Click the file you want to attach, and then click **A**ttach. Click Cl**o**se when you are finished selecting files. Click the **S**end button to send the fax.
Read a fax	Open the Inbox folder and double-click the fax message.
Print a fax from the Mail Program	Click the fax you want to print. Pull down the **F**ile menu and choose **P**rint. Click OK.
Print a fax attachment	Double-click the fax that contains the attachment. Double-click the attachment icon to start the application and open the file. Pull down the **F**ile menu and choose **P**rint.

On Your Own
Estimated time: 20 minutes

1. Start the Mail program. If necessary, connect to a post office. You may need to check with your system administrator for the necessary information. Confirm that a mail account has been set up for you.

2. Send a test message to the system administrator to verify that your mail system is working correctly.

3. Send a message to a coworker and have the coworker reply to your message.

4. Read the reply message.

5. Delete the reply message.

6. Send a message to a coworker that contains an attached file.

7. Create one or more message folders for future use.

8. If you have a fax/modem installed, configure the modem in Control Panel.

9. Send a fax from the Mail program.

11

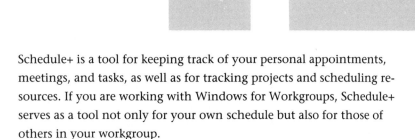

Using Schedule+

Schedule+ is a tool for keeping track of your personal appointments, meetings, and tasks, as well as for tracking projects and scheduling resources. If you are working with Windows for Workgroups, Schedule+ serves as a tool not only for your own schedule but also for those of others in your workgroup.

In this lesson, you learn how to

- Schedule a meeting

- Respond to a request for a meeting

- Read responses to your meeting request

- Reschedule a meeting

- Cancel a meeting

Schedule+ Basics

Schedule+ consists of three features—the Appointment Book, the Task List, and the Planner—that help you manage your own schedule and coordinate it with the schedules of other members of your workgroup.

The Appointment Book is your place in Schedule+ for assigning time-specific events, such as appointments and meetings. In the Appointment Book, you can schedule one-time-only events or events that occur at regular intervals, such as weekly staff meetings.

The Task List is the place in Schedule+ to list anything you must accomplish that is not necessarily assigned to a specific time period. Essentially, the Task List is a "to-do" list of all the tasks you need to complete, either by a specific date or whenever you can.

The Schedule+ Planner displays the busy and free times in your schedule in a day-by-time grid, enabling you to view several days at a time. If you are working *on-line*—that is, if you are connected to the mail server on your network—you can view the busy and free times of others in your workgroup as well.

Task: Start Schedule+

You start Schedule+ from the Network group in Program Manager. Schedule+ relies on the Mail program to distribute and receive requests for meetings. The Mail address list is used for workgroup scheduling. Unless you are already signed in to Mail, you must sign in through Schedule+. To sign in, you must have a user account with Mail and know your mailbox name and password. (See Lesson 11, "Using Mail and PC Fax," for information on Mail.)

To start and sign in to Schedule+, follow these steps:

1. Double-click the Network group icon in Program Manager. The Network group appears.

You use the Schedule+ icon in the Network program group to open Schedule+.

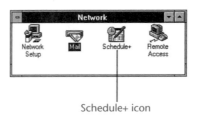

Schedule+ icon

2. Double-click the Schedule+ icon.

The Mail Sign In dialog box appears.

3. If necessary, type your mailbox name in the **M**ailbox text box.

4. Click **P**assword and type your mailbox password in the **P**assword text box. (As you type, asterisks rather than alphabetic characters appear in the text box, preventing anyone else from reading your password.)

5. Click OK.

Click here to return to your appointment schedule for today   The title bar displays your user name

After Schedule+ opens, the Schedule+ window displays the Appointment Book with the current date.

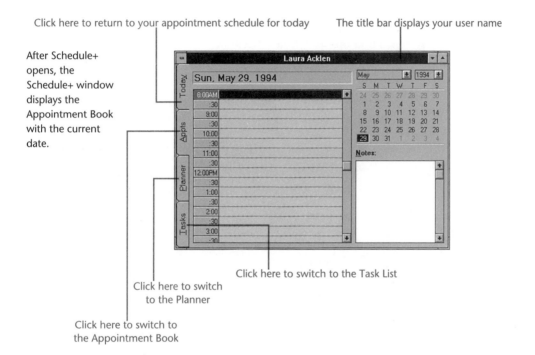

Click here to switch to the Task List

Click here to switch to the Planner

Click here to switch to the Appointment Book

Note: *If you are viewing someone else's schedule, you see that person's name in the title bar.*

When you sign in to Schedule+, you work on-line, which means that you are connected to your network's mail server. You can, for example, view the schedules of others in your workgroup and schedule meetings based on your coworkers' available time.

Task: Schedule a Meeting

When you schedule a meeting, you can select who you want to attend, and you can suggest a date and time for the meeting, based on times that appear to be open in the schedules of the people you want to attend. After you have scheduled a meeting, a request is sent to each invited group member.

You can attach a message to this request. Such a message might explain more about the agenda for the meeting. The request appears as a message in the Schedule+ Messages window as well as in the Inbox window in Mail. Each invited group member can then reply to your request by declining, accepting, or tentatively accepting the proposed meeting time. If those people respond with text messages, the responses appear in your Schedule+ Messages window and in your Mail Inbox.

To schedule a meeting, follow these steps:

1. Sign in to the Schedule+ program.

2. If your Planner is not already displayed, click the **P**lanner tab on the left side of the window.

A vertical line through a
time slot indicates an
appointment

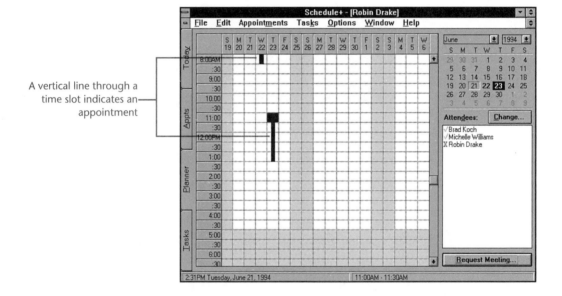

3. Note who is already listed in the Atten**d**ees list in the lower-right corner of the Planner window. If you want to select additional attendees, click the **C**hange button.

A check mark indicates that the person is
to be included in the meeting

Clicking a name in
the Attendees list
changes the marker
from a blank space
to either a check
mark or an X,
depending on
whether the person
has a conflict.

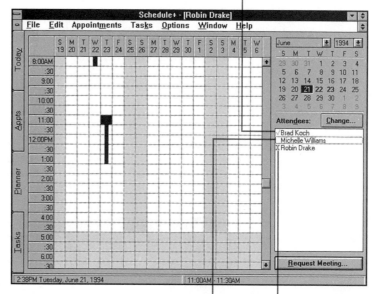

12

An X indicates that the person
has a scheduling conflict

If the marker is blank, the person has
not been included in the meeting

4. From the Attendees list, select the people that you want to attend
the meeting by clicking their names.

If you have problems...	If the list does not include the names of the people to whom you want to send a request, click the Directory button (the icon that looks like an open book), and select a new directory in the Open Directory dialog box. Click OK or press Enter. The Select Attendees dialog box appears.
If you have problems...	If the Planner's Attendees list includes people you don't want to attend, you can click their names in the Attendees list. As mentioned, a blank marker indicates that the person is not included in the meeting request. Now the schedules for these people are not shown in the Planner, and they are not sent a meeting request.

5. In the Planner, click on the beginning time for the proposed meeting and drag to the ending time for the meeting.

Be sure to select a time when everyone you want to attend is available. As mentioned, you can tell whether there are conflicts with your meeting time by the X marker next to a person's name in the Attendees list.

Note: *To quickly find a time when everyone in your Attendees list is available, select a time slot in the grid equal to the length of time for which you have scheduled the meeting. Then open the Appointments menu and either choose **A**uto-Pick or press Ctrl+A.*

6. Click the **R**equest Meeting button.

The Send Request
dialog box appears.

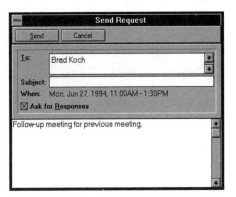

7. In the Subject text box, type a brief subject for the meeting. The subject you type here is also used as the description of the appointment in everyone's Appointment Book.

8. By default, the recipients of your request are asked to respond. If you don't want a response, deselect the Ask for **R**esponses check box.

9. Click in the message area and type a message to accompany the request. This step is optional.

10. Click the **S**end button.

A message box appears, informing you that the meeting was successfully booked. Click OK to return to the Planner. A hand-shaking icon is displayed next to meetings in your Appointment Book.

If the people that you ask to attend a meeting reply affirmatively, the meeting time is automatically marked in the Planners of all the invited attendees.

Task: Respond to a Scheduled Event

If someone else in your workgroup sends a request asking you to attend a meeting, you receive the request in your Schedule+ Messages window as well as in your Mail Inbox. You can read and respond to such requests in the Messages window.

To read and respond to meeting requests, follow these steps:

1. Sign in to Schedule+.

2. Pull down the **W**indow menu and choose Messages.

3. Double-click the request to which you want to respond.

You can accept, decline, or tentatively accept a meeting request in the Meeting Request window.

4. Click the View **S**chedule button to view your schedule.

5. Pull down the **W**indow menu and choose Meeting Request to return to the Meeting Request window.

6. Click **A**ccept, **D**ecline, or **T**entative. If you choose to accept or tentatively accept the request, Schedule+ enters the meeting in your Appointment Book.

After you choose the **A**ccept or **T**entative button, the Send Response window appears.

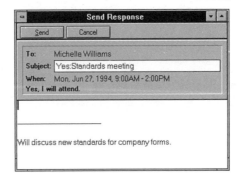

7. Click in the message area and type any message you want to add to your response.

8. Click the **S**end button.

Task: Read Responses to Your Meeting Request

After others respond to your meeting requests, their responses appear in the Schedule+ Messages window as well as in your Mail Inbox.

To read responses to your meeting request, follow these steps:

1. Sign in to Schedule+.

2. Pull down the **W**indow menu and choose Messages.

The Messages window appears.

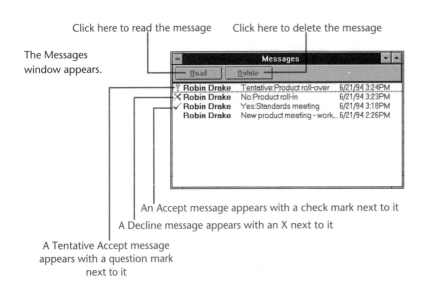

Click here to read the message

Click here to delete the message

An Accept message appears with a check mark next to it

A Decline message appears with an X next to it

A Tentative Accept message appears with a question mark next to it

3. Double-click the response you want to read. Then click the **R**ead button.

4. To delete a response, click the response and then click **D**elete.

Task: Reschedule a Meeting

No matter how well you plan, there will be occasions when you need to reschedule a meeting.

To reschedule a meeting, follow these steps:

1. Sign in to Schedule+.

2. If you are not already in your schedule window, pull down the **W**indow menu and click your name.

3. If your Appointment Book is not already displayed, choose the **A**ppts tab on the left side of the window.

4. Find the meeting in your Appointment Book. Click and drag the appointment to the time slot you prefer for the meeting.

You reschedule a meeting by dragging the appointment in the Appointment Book.

Note: *Alternatively, you can select the appointment, pull down the **E**dit menu, and choose Mo**v**e Appt (or press Ctrl+O). Then select the new time and date for the meeting from the Move Appointment dialog box.*

5. At this point, Schedule+ displays a dialog box that asks whether you want to notify the meeting's attendees of the change. Click **Y**es to display the Meeting Request window.

6. If you want, you can add a message to the updated request.

7. Click the **S**end button.

Attendees receive a new meeting request with the new time, to which they can respond as with any previous meeting request.

Task: Cancel a Meeting

At times, you may need to cancel a meeting you have scheduled.

To cancel a meeting, follow these steps:

1. Sign in to Schedule+.

2. If you are not already in your schedule window, open the **W**indow menu and select your name, or press the number key designated for your name.

3. If your Appointment Book is not already displayed, choose the **A**ppts tab on the left side of the window.

4. Click the meeting in your Appointment Book.

5. Pull down the **E**dit menu and choose **D**elete Appt.

   Note: *Alternatively, you can press Ctrl+D to delete a selected appointment.*

6. A message box asks whether you want to notify the meeting's attendees of the cancellation. Click **Y**es to display the Cancel Meeting window.

The subject is filled with Canceled, followed by the original subject.

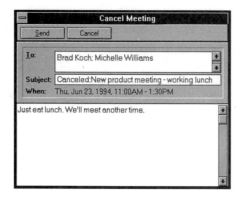

12

7. Type a message in the message area and click the **S**end button.

All attendees of the meeting receive a message notifying them of the cancellation. Schedule+ removes the meeting from all Appointment Books and Planners.

Task: Exit Schedule+

You can exit Schedule+ in one of two ways. You can quit Schedule+ but stay logged on to Mail, or you can exit Schedule+ and Mail with one command. To exit Schedule+ only, pull down the **F**ile menu and choose E**x**it. To exit both Schedule+ and Mail, pull down the **F**ile menu and choose Exi**t** and Sign Out.

Summary

To	Do This
Start the Schedule+ program	Double-click the Network group icon. Double-click the Schedule+ program icon. If necessary, type your mailbox name in the **M**ailbox text box. Type your mailbox password in the **P**assword text box. Click OK.
Schedule a meeting	If the Planner is not already displayed, click the **P**lanner tab. Note who is already listed in the Atten**d**ees list. If you want to add more attendees, click **C**hange. In the Planner, click on the beginning time and drag to the ending time. Click the **R**equest Meeting button. Type a subject in the

(continues)

To	Do This
	Subject text box. Click in the message area and type a message to accompany the meeting request. Click the **S**end button.
Respond to a scheduled event	Pull down the **W**indow menu and choose Messages. Double-click the request to which you want to respond. Choose the View **S**chedule button to view your schedule. Pull down the **W**indow menu and choose Meeting Request to return to the Meeting Request window. Click **A**ccept, **D**ecline, or **T**entative. If necessary, click in the message area and type a response. Click **S**end.
Read responses to your meeting request	Pull down the **W**indow menu and choose Messages. Double-click the response you want to read, and click the **R**ead button. If you want, click the response and then click **D**elete.
Reschedule a meeting	If you are not already in your schedule window, pull down the **W**indow menu and click your name. If necessary, click the **A**ppts tab to display your Appointment Book. Find the meeting you want to reschedule. Click and drag the meeting entry to a new time slot. Click **Y**es to notify the attendees of the change. If you want, type a short message explaining the change. Click **S**end.
Cancel a meeting	If you are not already in your schedule window, pull down the **W**indow menu and click your name. If necessary, click the **A**ppts tab to display your Appointment Book. Click the meeting you want to delete. Pull down the **E**dit menu and choose **D**elete Appt. Click **Y**es to notify the meeting's attendees. Type a message explaining the cancellation. Click **S**end.
Exit Schedule+ and stay logged on to Mail	Pull down the **F**ile menu and choose E**x**it.
Exit both Schedule+ and Mail	Pull down the **F**ile menu and choose Exi**t** and Sign Out.

On Your Own
Estimated time: 15 minutes

1. Sign in to Schedule+.

2. Schedule a test meeting (for example, lunch) with several of your coworkers.

3. Use the Auto-Pick feature to find an open time slot for your coworkers.

4. Have one of your coworkers request a meeting with you so that you can respond to the request.

5. Reschedule your lunch meeting to another day and notify your coworkers of the change.

6. Use the **W**indow menu to view the schedules of your coworkers.

12

Installing and Configuring DOS Applications

DOS applications are designed for the DOS environment, not the Windows environment. However, many DOS applications can be run from Windows. These applications are called *non-Windows applications* because they do not follow the Windows standards. To run a DOS application efficiently, you need to supply Windows with specific information about that program.

This lesson explains what you need to know about setting up and running DOS-based applications in the Windows environment. Specifically, you learn how to

- Start DOS programs from Program Manager and File Manager

- Set up a DOS application with the Setup program

- Create and edit program information files (PIFs) with PIF Editor

- Interpret PIF Editor options

- Toggle between full-screen and window operating modes while running a DOS application

- Switch between DOS programs

Running DOS Applications in Windows

Windows gives DOS programs, such as Lotus 1-2-3 for DOS and WordPerfect for DOS, more capabilities than they have when running under DOS. With Windows, you can run more than one DOS program at a time, as well as copy and paste text or numbers to other DOS or Windows programs.

You can create program icons for DOS programs with the same methods used to create icons for Windows programs.

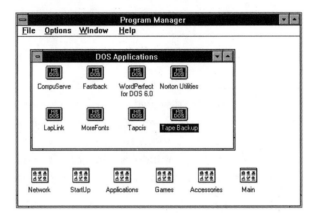

Although DOS programs gain features under Windows, DOS programs running under Windows do not have all the features of programs designed for Windows. Windows features not available to DOS programs include standardized menus, dialog boxes for quick access to options, better memory use, linking to pass data between programs, and embedding one program's data into another program's document.

In addition, DOS programs use their own screen and printer drivers. Even if you run a DOS program under Windows, the program cannot use the screens or printer drivers shared by Windows programs. Nor can DOS programs take advantage of Print Manager's capability to queue print jobs so that you can go back to work while Print Manager controls printing.

Starting DOS Applications

You can start DOS programs the same way you start Windows programs—from an icon in Program Manager or from a file in File Manager.

You can also open a DOS command window and run the program from the DOS prompt.

Note: *When you are running Windows, do not run DOS utilities or programs that modify files or the file allocation table. Such programs, while running, may modify the temporary files that Windows leaves open for its use. If the utilities and programs destroy or modify the temporary files, Windows may freeze, you may lose data, and you may need to reinstall Windows. These programs include Mace Utilities, Norton Utilities, and PC Tools, as well as the DOS CHKDSK command when used with the /F switch.*

Task: Start DOS Programs from Program Manager

Starting a DOS program from Program Manager is no different from starting a Windows program. The program icon assigned to all DOS programs looks like a blue computer screen with *MS-DOS* in the middle. You can change the icon to something more descriptive if you like (see the section "Task: Change an Icon" in Lesson 3).

Follow these steps to start a DOS program from Program Manager:

1. Open the group window that contains the program icon.

2. If necessary, scroll through the group window to locate the program item icon.

3. Double-click the program icon.

In this example, the program item icon for WordPerfect (in the DOS Applications group) is selected.

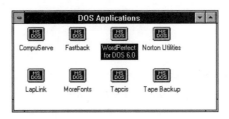

PIF

A program information file, containing the characteristics that determine how Windows works when a specific DOS program runs.

Task: Start DOS Programs from File Manager

You can start a DOS program also from File Manager. Open File Manager and then open the directory that contains the program file or the *PIF* (program information file) for the program. Program file names have the extension COM, EXE, or BAT.

13

Follow these steps to start a DOS program from File Manager:

1. Double-click the File Manager icon in the Main group window.

2. Select the drive where the program files are installed.

3. Open the directory where the program files are installed.

4. If necessary, scroll through the file list to locate the program file or PIF.

In this example, the PIF for WordPerfect 6.0 is selected.

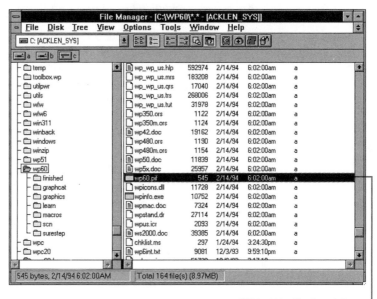

PIF for WordPerfect 6.0

5. Double-click the file name to start the program.

Note: *For more information on File Manager, see Lesson 7, "Displaying and Organizing Files," and Lesson 8, "Managing Files, Directories, and Disks."*

Task: Set Up DOS Applications

During a standard installation of Windows, the Setup program searches your hard disk for existing applications and sets up those applications in Windows for you. Setup creates program item icons and group windows for both DOS and Windows programs. Setup searches for a PIF for each of your DOS applications and, if necessary, creates one based on information provided by Windows. If you install applications later, you can run the Setup program at any time to add those applications to Windows.

To set up a DOS program in Windows, follow these steps:

1. Double-click the Windows Setup icon in the Main group window.

2. Pull down the **O**ptions menu and choose **S**et Up Applications.

The Set Up
Applications dialog
box appears.

3. Click either the Search for Applications option or the Ask You to Specify an Application option.

4. Click OK.

5. If you selected Ask You to Specify an Application, a different Set Up Applications dialog box appears. Type the program path and file name in the text box; then choose from the **A**dd to Program Group list box the name of the group window where you want to add the program item. (If you do not know the name of the file or path, click the **B**rowse button and select the file name of the program.) Click OK twice to complete the setup. (You can skip steps 6 and 7.)

In this Set Up
Applications dialog
box, you type the
full path of the
program file and
specify the group
window where you
want to add the
program.

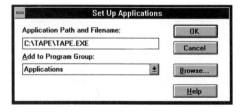

DOS path
A list of directories
specified in the
AUTOEXEC.BAT file.

6. If you selected Search for Applications, a different Set Up Applications dialog box appears. In the Setup Will Search list box, select the *DOS path* and/or drive(s). Then click the **S**earch Now button.

As Windows searches for DOS programs, it may ask you to identify a program. For example, if Windows asks you to identify WP.EXE, select WordPerfect from the list. If Windows suggests the wrong program for the file, select None of the Above from the list box.

You can have Windows search the DOS path specified in your AUTOEXEC.BAT file and/or available drives.

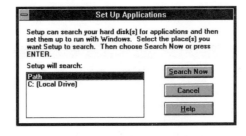

When the search is complete, another Set Up Applications dialog box appears.

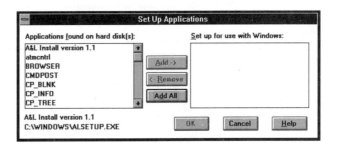

7. Click **A**dd All to set up all the listed programs. Or, from the list on the left side of the dialog box, select the programs you want to add to Windows; then click **A**dd to add those programs to the list box on the right. Click OK to complete the setup process.

If you have problems...

If there is a naming conflict or multiple PIFs for one application, you will need to specify the name of the application or the PIF you want to use.

If you click **A**dd All and then decide that you don't want to set up all those programs, highlight the ones you don't want in the list on the right, and then click **R**emove.

8. If Setup doesn't find a PIF for a selected DOS application, it searches for the information needed to create one. If the information is found, a dialog box appears asking whether you want Setup to use this information. When you click Yes, a PIF is created.

Creating and Editing PIFs

A PIF determines how Windows works when you run a specific DOS program. During the Windows installation process, the Setup program automatically creates PIFs for your DOS programs. If Windows could not create a PIF for a DOS program, Windows runs that program using the settings in a default PIF.

In a few cases, Windows cannot run a DOS program with the default PIF settings. For these programs, you must create a custom PIF with PIF Editor. If your programs will not run correctly or as efficiently as you want, you can edit the PIF with PIF Editor.

Task: Create a PIF

When Windows is unable to create a PIF for one of your DOS programs, you will need to create the PIF manually with PIF Editor.

13

To create a new PIF, follow these steps:

1. Double-click the PIF Editor icon in the Main group window.

In the Main group window, the PIF Editor icon looks like a tag.

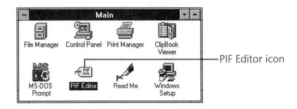

When you start PIF Editor, a window displays a new, untitled PIF with the default settings.

2. Type information in the text boxes and select options. See table 13.1 for more information on the individual options.

3. Pull down the **F**ile menu and choose **S**ave.

4. Type a name (up to eight characters) in the File **N**ame text box.

5. Click OK to save the file.

6. To close PIF Editor, pull down the **F**ile menu and choose E**x**it.

Caution

Before testing a PIF, close all other programs in Windows. That way, if the program freezes the system, you can turn off the computer and restart it without losing data in another program.

If you plan to start the program by choosing the program file name, the PIF must have the same name as the program file (such as WP.EXE and WP.PIF). Then, when you choose the program file name, Windows executes the PIF. If you have several WordPerfect PIFs (for the same WordPerfect program) with different settings, start the program by choosing the PIF.

Table 13.1 PIF Editor Options

Option	Description
Program Filename	Use this option to specify the full path name and DOS program name, including the file extension. Most programs have the extension EXE or COM. Batch files that run commands or start programs have the extension BAT. For example, for WordPerfect 6.0, use C:\WP60\WP.EXE.
Window **T**itle	Use this option to specify the name that will appear in the program window title bar and under the program item icon.
Optional Parameters	Use this option to specify the parameters that will be added to the program when it starts (the parameters or switches that you type after the file name when you start the program from the DOS prompt). For example, if you type **/m-*macroname*,** the specified macro starts when you start WordPerfect 6.0. If you frequently change program startup parameters, type a question mark (?) for **O**ptional Parameters. Then Windows prompts you for the parameters you want to use when it starts the program.
Start-up Directory	Use this option to specify the full path name of the drive and directory where you want Windows to go when the program starts. If the program needs to locate additional files at startup (as does Lotus 1-2-3), make sure that you indicate a start-up directory that is the same as the program's directory.

Option	Description
Video Memory	Windows allocates memory to display the application in the video mode you specify. Text mode uses the least amount of memory; High Graphics mode uses the most. Select the highest mode your program will use. In addition, non-Text mode applications should have the Retain Video Memory setting checked in the **A**dvanced section.
Memory Requirements KB **R**equired	Type the minimum amount of conventional memory the application requires. If you don't know how much is required, leave the setting alone. Application manuals usually specify too much free memory because they must include memory for DOS and drivers. Windows will not start the program if the KB **R**equired setting is not large enough. Use a setting of -1 to give the program all available conventional memory.
Memory Requirements KB **D**esired	Type the maximum amount of conventional memory your program can use, if memory is available; 640K is the maximum. Most programs use much less. Using a smaller setting conserves memory. Some programs run more efficiently with more memory. Use a setting of -1 to give the program as much memory as possible, but not more than 640K.
EMS Memory **K**B Required	Type the minimum amount of expanded memory your application requires. If you don't know how much is required, leave the setting alone. Use a setting of 0 for applications that don't use expanded memory.
EMS Memory KB **L**imit	Type the maximum amount of expanded memory you want allocated to this application. This option prevents an application from taking more memory than it needs. A setting of -1 allocates as much memory as the application requests, up to the limit of system memory (this can slow down the rest of your system). A setting of 0 prevents the application from using expanded memory.
XMS Memory KB Re**q**uired	Type the minimum amount of extended memory your application requires. If you don't know how much is required, leave the setting alone. Use a setting of 0 for applications that don't use extended memory.

13

(continues)

Table 13.1 Continued	
Option	**Description**
XMS Memory KB Limit	Type the maximum amount of extended memory you want allocated to this application. Use this setting to prevent an application from reserving all available extended memory blocks. A setting of -1 allocates as much extended memory to an application as it requests, up to the limit of system memory (this can slow down the rest of your system). A setting of 0 prevents an application from using extended memory (except the high memory area).
Display Usage Full Screen	Use this option to start the program full-screen.
Display Usage Windowed	Use this option to start the program in a window.
Execution Background	Use this option to run the program while you are using another program. When this option is selected, programs running in the background share processing power with programs running in the foreground.
Execution Exclusive	Use this option to stop all other programs while this program is active. This option gives a program more computer power.
Close Window on Exit	Use this option to close the window when you exit the program.
Advanced	Click the Advanced button to display the Advanced Options dialog box. For a detailed discussion of the advanced options, see Que's *Using Windows*, 3.11 Edition, Special Edition.

Task: Edit a PIF

Windows Setup can create predefined PIFs for many popular DOS programs. Some DOS programs include a PIF with the program. The PIF is optimized for that particular program, so you should always use the PIF included with the program. You can make adjustments at any time with PIF Editor.

Note: *Before you edit a PIF, make sure that you make a backup copy of the original PIF. For example, for a WordPerfect PIF such as WP.PIF, you might use the backup name WP.BAK. If your edited PIF causes problems, you can return to the preceding version by renaming the backup copy with the original name.*

Follow these steps to edit an existing PIF:

1. Double-click the PIF Editor icon in the Main group window.

2. Pull down the **F**ile menu and choose **O**pen.

3. Change to the directory containing the PIF you want to edit. PIFs are usually in the Windows directory. Select and open the PIF you want to edit.

   The PIF Editor window displays the PIF for that program.

4. Pull down the **F**ile menu and choose Save **A**s. Save a backup copy of the PIF by replacing the PIF extension with a BAK extension.

5. Pull down the **F**ile menu and choose Save **A**s again. This time, save the file under the original name by replacing the BAK extension with the PIF extension.

13

In this example, the PIF for WordPerfect 6.0 is open.

```
┌─────────────────────────────────────────────────────┐
│  ▭          PIF Editor - WP60.PIF              ▼ ▲   │
│ File   Mode   Help                                  │
│ Program Filename:    │WP.COM                      │  │
│ Window Title:        │WordPerfect for DOS 6.0     │  │
│ Optional Parameters: │                            │  │
│ Start-up Directory:  │                            │  │
│ Video Memory:    ⦿ Text   ○ Low Graphics  ○ High Graphics │
│ Memory Requirements:  KB Required  │480│  KB Desired │640│ │
│ EMS Memory:           KB Required  │0│    KB Limit  │-1│  │
│ XMS Memory:           KB Required  │0│    KB Limit  │-1│  │
│ Display Usage: ⦿ Full Screen   Execution: ☐ Background │
│                ○ Windowed                 ☐ Exclusive │
│ ☒ Close Window on Exit    │ Advanced... │           │
│ Press F1 for Help on Program Filename.              │
└─────────────────────────────────────────────────────┘
```

6. Make changes to the text boxes or selections in the PIF Editor window. (See table 13.1 earlier for detailed descriptions of the available options.)

7. Pull down the **F**ile menu and choose **S**ave to save your changes.

8. Pull down the **F**ile menu and choose E**x**it to quit PIF Editor.

Controlling DOS Programs

Windows enables you to run multiple DOS programs, switch from one program to another, and copy and paste text and numbers between programs. See Lesson 14, "Sharing Data between Applications," for more information on copying and pasting text between DOS and Windows programs.

You can run most DOS applications in a window. If you prefer, you can modify the PIF so that the application runs in a window every time you start it, by selecting the **W**indowed option from the PIF Editor dialog box.

You can also switch a DOS application between full-screen and a window. Double-click the DOS application's program icon in the appropriate group window to start the program. If the program is running full-screen, press Alt+Enter to switch to a window. If the program is running in a window, press Alt+Enter to switch to full-screen.

Windows uses the same key combinations to switch between programs, regardless of whether they are Windows or DOS programs. To switch from an active DOS program to another program, press Alt+Tab until you see the window or name of the program you want to activate.

Another way to switch between programs is to use the Task List. To minimize a full-screen DOS program to an icon and display the Task List so that you can activate a different program, press Ctrl+Esc.

Some DOS programs prevent keyboard use in some operating modes; therefore, Alt+Tab (to switch between programs) and Ctrl+Esc (to activate the Task List) may not work. To switch back to Windows, return to the program's normal operating mode and then press Alt+Tab or Ctrl+Esc. If, for example, you are displaying a graph in 1-2-3 Release 2.2, press Esc to return to the worksheet or menu, and then press Alt+Tab or Ctrl+Esc.

Summary

To	Do This
Start a DOS program from Program Manager	Open the group window that contains the program icon. Double-click the program item icon.
Start a DOS program from File Manager	Double-click the File Manager icon in the Main group window. Select the drive and directory where a DOS application is installed. Double-click the program file.
Set up a DOS application	Double-click the Windows Setup icon in the Main group window. Pull down the **O**ptions menu and choose **S**et Up Applications. Choose either to specify an application or to have Setup search for applications. Click OK. If you choose to specify an application, type the full path and file name for the program file and then choose a group window in which to place the program icon. Click OK twice to complete the setup. If you choose to have Setup search for applications, select the application from the list and click **A**dd; or click A**d**d All to set up all the listed applications. Click OK to complete the setup process.
Create a PIF	Double-click the PIF Editor icon in the Main group window. Type the information in the text boxes and select the appropriate options. Pull down the **F**ile menu and choose **S**ave. Type a file name in the File **N**ame text box. Click OK. Pull down the **F**ile menu and choose E**x**it to quit the PIF Editor program.
Edit a PIF	Double-click the PIF Editor icon in the Main group window. Pull down the **F**ile menu and choose **O**pen. Select a PIF file from the list. Make the necessary adjustments. Pull down the **F**ile menu and choose **S**ave to save your changes. Pull down the **F**ile menu and choose E**x**it to quit the PIF Editor program.
Switch a DOS application between full-screen and a window	Double-click the DOS program icon in the appropriate group window. Press Alt+Enter to toggle between full-screen and a window.
Switch between DOS programs	Use Alt+Tab or Ctrl+Esc (Task List). If these keystrokes don't work, restore the DOS application to its normal editing state and try the keystrokes again.

13

On Your Own
Estimated time: 15 minutes

1. Use File Manager to start a DOS application on your system.

2. Use the Setup program to search for applications on your system. Choose an application that is not already assigned to an icon in Windows and have the Setup program set it up for you. Then run the program from the icon. After you exit the program, if you don't want to keep the program item icon for that program, delete it.

3. Start the PIF Editor program and open a PIF for one of your DOS applications. (*Hint:* Use **B**rowse to look for a PIF on your system.) Read through the current settings. Exit PIF Editor *without saving changes* to the PIF.

4. Start a DOS application. Toggle between full-screen and a window.

Sharing Data between Applications

Often, one program is better than another at handling certain kinds of information. Spreadsheets handle columns of numbers, do complicated analysis and calculations, and create graphs with ease. Drawing programs give you lots of options for building logos, importing pictures, and painting colorful graphics. Word processing programs are great with text. But real-world documents sometimes require combining these functions. You may need graphics in your annual report or tables of sales figures in a newsletter.

One of the most useful features of Windows is its capability to run multiple programs—both Windows and DOS programs—at the same time and to transfer data between those programs. Windows enables you to use different Windows programs as though they were parts of a single program. By integrating programs, you multiply their power, making your work more efficient and your results more professional.

This lesson discusses the different methods available for sharing data between DOS and Windows applications. Specifically, you learn to

- Paste data and graphics between Windows programs

- Copy information from a DOS program to a Windows program and from a Windows program to a DOS program

- Copy information between DOS programs

- Link two Windows applications

Pasting Data

One of the easiest ways to transfer data between programs is to use the copy and paste operations common to all Windows programs. To do this, you select the data you want to copy from one Windows program, pull down the **E**dit menu and choose **C**opy, switch to the other Windows program, position the insertion point where you want to place that data, and pull down the **E**dit menu and choose **P**aste. (If you are working with DOS programs, however, you must perform additional steps; and when you copy formatted text, the formatting will be lost when the text is pasted.)

Nearly all Windows programs contain Cu**t**, **C**opy, and **P**aste commands on the **E**dit menu. These commands enable you to cut or copy information you have selected in one place and to paste it somewhere else. You can use these techniques to copy and move information within a document, between documents, or between programs. The operations for cutting and copying are almost identical, but the results are different:

- ■ *Cutting.* Removes selected text or graphics from a program and stores the text or graphics. You use the cut operation to *move* text or graphics. The information can then be inserted (pasted) in another location.

- ■ *Copying.* Stores a duplicate of selected text or graphics from a program. You use the copy operation to *copy* text or graphics. The information can then be inserted (pasted) in another location.

Clipboard

An area of memory reserved to hold text or graphics that you cut or copy.

An important part of the copying and moving process is the *Clipboard.* Like a writer's clipboard, the Clipboard is a Windows program that holds information so that you can copy or move it from one place to another—within *and* between programs.

Because copying information between programs is fairly new, at first you may not think of many ways to use the feature. But as you work more with multiple programs, you will find that copying and pasting between programs saves you time, eliminates typing errors, and gives you the chance to use programs together as though they were part of a single program. The following task takes you through a short exercise in using the Clipboard for simple data sharing between applications.

Note: *If you are using Windows for Workgroups, you will use the Clipbook instead of the Clipboard for cut, copy, and paste operations. The Clipbook works like the Clipboard, but the Clipbook can also store data for future use and allow it to be shared with other users in the workgroup.*

To refresh your memory about switching between programs, refer to Lesson 4, "Starting and Controlling Applications."

Task: Copy a Picture into a Letter

In this example, you open a picture file in the Windows Paintbrush program and copy that picture into a letter in Write (refer to Lesson 10, "Using Write," for a review of the Write program).

Follow these steps to copy and paste information between Windows programs:

1. Start the Write program.

2. Type today's date and press Enter three times.

3. Type the following text (do not press Enter at the end of each line, only at the end of the paragraph):

   > I have discovered the Windows logo in some of the files included with the program. I would like to use the logo as a sample file in our training classes.

The Write program shows a sample letter.

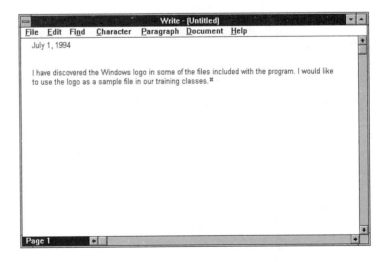

14

4. Press Ctrl+Esc to open the Task List. Double-click Program Manager to return to Program Manager.

5. Open the Accessories group.

6. Double-click the Paintbrush program icon.

7. Pull down the **F**ile menu and choose **O**pen.

8. Scroll down to the bottom of the file list and double-click the WINLOGO.BMP file.

The WINLOGO.BMP file is in the Paintbrush program.

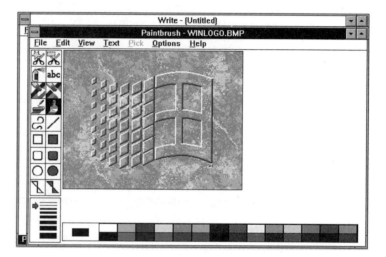

9. Click the tool in the upper-right corner of the toolbar. This is the Pick tool.

10. Point to the lower-right corner of the logo picture. The arrow pointer changes to a crosshair pointer.

If you have problems...   If you can't get the mouse pointer to stay as a cross, be patient. Move the pointer slowly back and forth over the corner.

---

11. Click and drag the mouse to the upper-left corner of the picture to select the whole picture.

You can use the
mouse to select the
part of the picture
you want to copy.

A dotted guide line
marks your selection as —
you drag the mouse

When you click the mouse,
the pointer changes back to —
the standard pointer

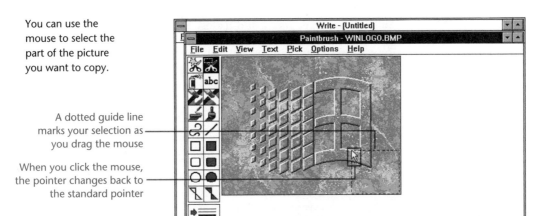

12. Pull down the **E**dit menu and choose **C**opy.

13. Pull down the **F**ile menu and choose E**x**it to exit the Paintbrush program.

14. Switch back to the Write program. If necessary, position the insertion point at the bottom of the text you typed. Press Enter three times.

15. Pull down the **E**dit menu and choose **P**aste.

14

The picture from
Paintbrush is
copied into your
letter.

Sample letter

Picture copied —
from Paintbrush

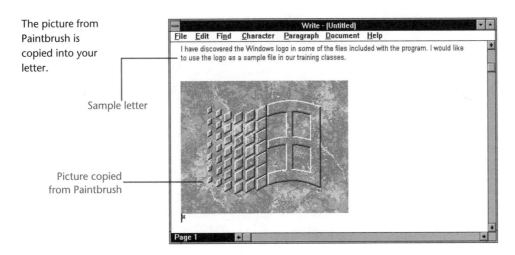

16. Pull down the **F**ile menu and choose **S**ave.

17. Type **winlogo.wri** in the File **N**ame text box.

18. Exit the Write program.

Sharing Data between DOS and Windows

DOS programs can use the copy-and-paste capability provided by Windows, but there are some limitations. You can paste text or graphics from DOS programs into Windows programs; however, only Windows programs designed to work with graphics will receive graphics. For more information on running DOS programs under Windows, refer to Lesson 13, "Installing and Configuring DOS Applications."

Moving text in DOS programs is different from moving text in Windows programs. In DOS programs running under Windows, you do not have a cut command as you do in Windows programs. To move text from a DOS program running under Windows, you must copy and paste the text using the Windows technique, and then delete the text from the DOS program using the program's own technique.

Task: Copy from a DOS Program to a Windows Program

Running a DOS program in a window gives you access to the Control menu. The Control menu commands enable you to mark and copy selected text. If you want, you can copy the DOS screen (full-screen or a window) to the Clipboard.

Note: *The DOS program should be running in a window—not full-screen—for you to copy selected text.*

Follow these steps to copy selected text from a DOS program and paste it into a Windows program:

1. If the DOS program is running full-screen, put the program in a window by pressing Alt+Enter.

2. Open the document that contains the text you want to copy.

3. Click the Control menu box at the upper-left corner of the window and then choose the **E**dit command.

The Control Edit menu contains the Windows commands to mark, copy, and paste information.

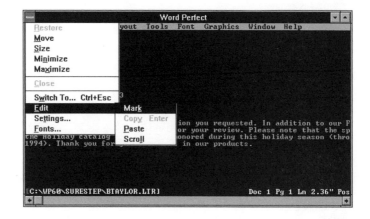

4. Choose the Mar**k** command.

5. Select the text you want to copy by pointing to a corner of the area you want to select, holding down the mouse button, and dragging across the area.

Select appears in the title bar of the window

Selected text in a DOS program appears in reverse video.

Selected text—

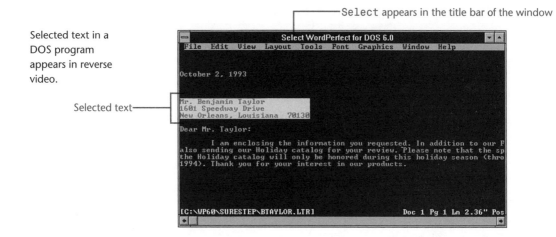

14

6. Click the right mouse button to copy the selected text to the Clipboard.

Note: *While you are selecting text with the mouse, the title bar of the program changes to show the word* Select. *You can't paste or use the program while you are selecting. Press Esc to return to program control.*

7. You can press Alt+Enter a second time to restore the DOS program to full-screen if you like.

8. Switch to the Windows program where you want to paste the text or graphics.

9. Open the document in which you want to insert the copied text.

10. Place the insertion point where you want to paste the text or graphics.

11. Pull down the **E**dit menu and choose **P**aste.

The information from WordPerfect (the DOS program) has been pasted into Write (the Windows program).

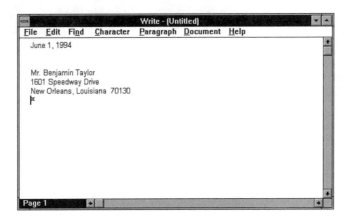

Note: *To copy a graphics screen from a DOS program, press PrtSc or Alt+PrtSc. The entire screen or window is copied to the Clipboard.*

Task: Copy from a Windows Program to a DOS Program

Running DOS programs in a window gives you access to the Control menu. The Control menu commands enable you to paste text from a Windows program. You can paste formatted text into DOS programs, but only the text will be pasted (the formatting will be stripped out).

Note: *The DOS program should be running in a window—not full-screen—for you to paste text.*

Follow these steps to copy selected text from a Windows program and paste it into a DOS program:

1. Switch to the Windows program and open the document containing the text you want to copy.

2. Select the text.

3. Pull down the **E**dit menu and choose **C**opy.

4. Switch to the DOS program.

5. If the DOS program is running full-screen, put the program in a window by pressing Alt+Enter.

6. Open the document in which you want to insert the copied text.

7. Position the cursor where you want to paste the text.

8. Click the Control menu box at the upper-left corner of the window and choose the **E**dit command.

9. Choose **P**aste.

Task: Share Data between DOS Programs

Windows makes it possible to share data between DOS programs. Although there are DOS programs that make this possible, the process is awkward, and the results can be inconsistent.

To copy and paste text between DOS programs, follow these steps:

1. If the DOS program from which you want to copy is running full-screen, put the program in a window by pressing Alt+Enter.

2. Open the document that contains the text you want to copy.

3. Click the Control menu box at the upper-left corner of the window and choose the **E**dit command.

4. Choose Mar**k**.

5. Select the text you want to copy.

6. Click the right mouse button to copy the selected text to the Clipboard.

7. Switch to the DOS program where you want to paste the text. If this DOS program is running full-screen, put the program in a window by pressing Alt+Enter.

8. Open the document in which you want to insert the copied text.

9. Position the cursor where you want to paste the text.

10. Click the Control menu box at the upper-left corner of the window and choose the **E**dit command.

11. Choose **P**aste.

14

Linking and Embedding Data

Source

The document that contains the information you want to cut or copy.

Destination

The document in which you want to paste the cut or copied information.

Server

An application that creates objects which can be linked or embedded by a client application.

Client

An application capable of receiving linked or embedded objects.

Object

In OLE, a document or portion of a document that has been pasted into another document.

Copying and pasting data from the Clipboard is somewhat limited. When you use the standard method, there is no tie between the *source* and *destination* documents. If you make a change in the source document, you must make the same change in the destination document to keep it current, or repeat the copy and paste operation so that you will be pasting the most current version of the text.

With Object Linking and Embedding (OLE), however, you can create a *dynamic link* between the source and destination documents. Linking and embedding provide the greatest level of integration between Windows programs. Although the methods are similar, the results are quite different:

- *Linking* enables Windows to transfer any updated data from the *server* application to the *client* application. When you make changes in the source document, those changes are reflected in the destination document. Windows can transfer the changes automatically or when you request an update. Some programs function as both server and client applications; others are only one or the other.

  If an *object* is linked to multiple documents (or even multiple programs), the object can be modified from within *any* document. When the object is modified, each document containing a link to that object is updated. Linking thus makes it easy to track information that appears in more than one place and that must be identical.

- *Embedding* "buries" one program's data within another program's document. The information in the destination document is independent of the information in the source document.

  Embedding is virtually the same as linking, except that a *copy* of the object is created and placed in the destination document. Because the object isn't linked to its original, changes can be made in any file containing the object without affecting any other file that contains the same object. Because the object is independent, the original file is not needed to maintain the link.

Note: *Some Windows applications, especially older ones, do not support OLE. If your application does not support OLE, you will not be able to create OLE links. You might be able to create DDE links, however. Consult your program documentation or system administrator to determine which of the two your program will support.*

If the document will be sent to other users, use embedding. Embedding places a copy of the object in the document and is saved as a part of the document. If a document containing a link is to be sent to other users, the source file must also be sent.

You still use the Clipboard to copy the information from the source document to the destination document, but the Paste Link and Paste Special commands on the **E**dit menu create a DDE or OLE Link, whereas the **O**bject command on the **I**nsert menu creates an embedded object.

Double-clicking either linked or embedded information loads the originating application; you can then edit the information.

Task: Create a Link between a Picture and a Letter

14

In this example, you paste the Paintbrush picture into the letter in Write with a Paste Link operation between the two programs. You then add some text to the graphic and watch the changes automatically reflected in the letter.

Follow these steps to create a Paste Link:

1. Start the Write program.

2. Open the WINLOGO.WRI file you previously created. If you do not have a WINLOGO.WRI file, refer to the section "Task: Copy a Picture into a Letter" earlier in this lesson for details on creating the file.

3. Click anywhere in the logo graphic. The graphic should turn to a darker gray.

4. Press the Del key to erase the graphic.

5. Switch back to Program Manager and start the Paintbrush program.

6. Open the WINLOGO.BMP file.

7. Click the Pick tool in the upper-right corner of the toolbar.

8. Point to the bottom-right corner of the logo picture. The mouse pointer changes to a crosshair pointer.

If you have problems...

If you can't get the mouse pointer to stay as a cross, be patient. Move the pointer slowly back and forth over the corner.

---

9. Click and drag the mouse to the upper-left corner of the picture to select the whole picture.

   As soon as you click the mouse, the pointer changes back to the standard pointer. You also see a dotted guide line marking your selection as you drag the mouse.

10. Pull down the **E**dit menu and choose **C**opy.

11. Switch back to the Write program. Place the insertion point at the bottom of the text you typed. Press Enter three times.

12. Pull down the **E**dit menu and choose Paste **L**ink.

The Paste **L**ink command links the object in Write (the Windows logo) to its originating application (Paintbrush).

Note: *If your application does not have a Paste Link command on the* **E***dit menu, you will not be able to create an Object Link. You can however, create an Object Embed if you have Paste Special on the* **E***dit menu. The only difference between the two is that an Object Link is updated automatically while the changes are taking place. An Object Embed will be updated on request. All you have to do is double-click the object to see the changes reflected.*

13. Use the Task List to close all programs except Paintbrush and Write.

14. Minimize Program Manager to an icon at the bottom of the screen.

15. Choose **T**ile from the Task List to tile the Paintbrush and Write programs on-screen.

16. Click in the Paintbrush window to make it active.

17. Click the Text tool, located below the Pick tool in the upper-right corner of the toolbar.

18. Click the bright blue box at the bottom of the Paintbrush window. If you have a monochrome monitor, click the black box at the bottom of the Paintbrush window.

19. Click in the upper-left corner of the WINLOGO graphic.

20. Type **We do Windows at BTA, Incorporated!**

Use the Paintbrush program to make modifications to the WINLOGO.BMP file.

Click here to make Paintbrush active

14

Click here to select the Text tool

Click here for blue text

If you watch carefully as you type, you will see that the characters appear in the graphic in the letter.

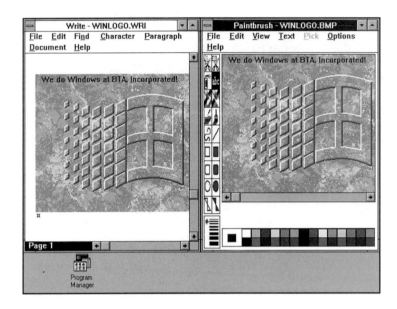

With an Object Link, the changes are reflected automatically, as you can see in the example. As you type the text in Paintbrush, it appears in the Write window. However, if you have created an Object Embed with Paste Special, you will need to double-click the object to see the changes.

Understanding DDE versus OLE

Dynamic Data Exchange (DDE) is a feature of many Windows programs that enables them to pass data to documents in other Windows programs supporting DDE. (These connections are often called *hot links*.) When you change data in the server application document, Windows sends those changes to each client application document.

Note: *Some Windows applications, especially older ones, do not support OLE. The alternative is Dynamic Data Exchange (DDE).*

When you create a link with Dynamic Data Exchange, the data in the destination document is physically linked to the data in the source docu ment. The data itself is not actually placed in the destination document. A pair of link codes, making the location where you want the data to be inserted, is placed in the destination document.

If changes are made in the source document, you will be notified when you start the client application and open the destination document. Then you can elect to update the link or not. If both applications are open and the source file was opened first, the updating will be automatic.

The primary difference between DDE and OLE is that OLE is newer and more sophisticated. OLE links automate the processing of loading the original (server) application and opening the source (object) file for editing. DDE links require that the editing process be done manually from the server application. because the data has not physically been placed in the destination file. With OLE, the data is actually placed in the source document and can be edited from there. With OLE links, you double-click the object in the client application to load the server application and open the source document for editing. This approach eliminates the need to switch between applications to view or change different kinds of information. All operations can be performed from one document.

Summary

To	Do This
Copy information between Windows programs	Select the text you want to copy. Pull down the **E**dit menu and choose **C**opy. Switch to the program where you want to paste the text. Position the insertion point, pull down the **E**dit menu, and choose **P**aste.
Copy from a DOS program to a Windows program	If the DOS program is running full-screen, press Alt+Enter. Open the source document and position the cursor at the beginning of the text you want to copy. Click the Control menu box, choose **E**dit, and then choose Mar**k.** Select the text you want to copy. Click the right mouse button to copy the text to the Clipboard. Switch to the Windows program and place the insertion point where you want the text to be inserted. Pull down the **E**dit menu and choose **P**aste.
Copy from a Windows program to a DOS program	Switch to the Windows program and place the insertion point at the beginning of the text you want to copy. Select the text. Pull down the **E**dit menu and choose **C**opy. Switch to the DOS program. If the DOS program is running full-screen, press Alt+Enter. Position the cursor where you want to paste the text. Click the Control menu box, choose **E**dit, and then choose **P**aste.
Copy between DOS programs	If the first DOS program is running full-screen, press Alt+Enter. Position the cursor at the beginning of the text to be copied. Click the Control menu box, choose Edit, and then choose Mark. Select the text you want to copy. Click the right mouse button to copy the text to

14

(continues)

To	Do This
	the Clipboard. Switch to the second DOS program. If this DOS program is running full-screen, press Alt+Enter. Position the cursor where you want to paste the text. Click the Control menu box, choose Edit, and then choose Paste.
Create a link	Start the Windows program. Select the object you want to copy. Pull down the **E**dit menu and choose **C**opy. Switch to the other Windows program. Place the insertion point where you want the object to be inserted. Pull down the **E**dit menu and choose Paste Link or Paste Special—whichever is available.

On Your Own
Estimated time: 25 minutes

1. Open two Windows programs—for example, Write and Notepad.

2. Type a short block of text in the Write program.

3. Select the text and copy it into Notepad.

4. Start a DOS word processing or spreadsheet program.

5. Open a file in the program.

6. Select a block of text or numbers to copy.

7. Paste the selection into the Write program.

8. If you have two DOS programs on your system, practice copying data between the two programs.

9. Start both the Write and Paintbrush programs.

10. Open a picture file in Paintbrush.

11. Select the picture and then paste it into the Write program by using the Paste Link operation.

12. Tile the Paintbrush and Write programs.

13. Make changes to the picture in Paintbrush and watch the changes reflected in the Write document.

Installing Windows 3.11 or Windows for Workgroups 3.11

This appendix shows you how to install Windows 3.11 or Windows for Workgroups 3.11. If either version is already installed on your computer, you can skip this appendix. Go right to Lesson 1, "Learning the Basics," to start learning Windows from the beginning. However, the information in this appendix may be helpful if you need to change Windows Setup after the initial installation.

Note: *Windows for Workgroups 3.11 installation is practically identical to Windows 3.11 installation. You must use Express Setup, however, if you are upgrading from a previous version of Windows to Windows for Workgroups Version 3.11.*

Pay close attention to the screen as you install or upgrade; the installation program may request permission to overwrite files, information on where you want files or programs placed, and so on.

Understanding the Setup Program

The Windows Setup program guides you through installing Windows. If you already have Windows 3.1 installed, you should install Windows 3.11 over the existing Windows. This procedure preserves your current settings, program groups, and custom drivers. Drivers for existing printers may be upgraded. Installation should take no more than 30 minutes.

Two Setup modes are available: Express and Custom. If you are unfamiliar with computers, you should use Express Setup. It determines your hardware and software and makes appropriate selections for you. You are prompted to specify which type of printer your computer uses and where it is connected.

If you are familiar with computers and want to install only parts of Windows or make changes during installation, you should use Custom Setup. Custom Setup enables you to select hardware that may be different from what is automatically detected by the Setup program, as well as select which applications you want added to Program Manager. If your hard disk is low on available storage, you may want to use Custom Setup to install parts of Windows rather than the full version of Windows and all accessories. You can run Setup at any time to add Windows features or accessories you did not install initially.

Windows 3.11 Requirements

For Windows to operate correctly, your hardware and software must meet the following requirements:

- IBM, COMPAQ, or compatible computer with a 386SX or higher processor if you are installing Windows for Workgroups 3.11. Windows 3.11 can run in Standard mode with a 286 processor.

- 3M or more of memory; 4M is recommended. Only 2M is required if you disable the networking capability. (You should configure memory above 640K as extended memory. Refer to your hardware installation manual for this information.)

- Graphics adapter card supported by Windows 3.1. A color VGA monitor or one with a higher resolution is recommended.

- Windows for Workgroups requires a minimum of 13M of free disk space or 18M if you install all the components. Upgrading over an earlier version of Windows for Workgroups reduces the requirement to a minumum of 3.5M or 8.5M if you install all the components. If you are upgrading over Windows 3.11, the minumum requirement is 6.5M or 9M to install all components.

Windows 3.11 requires a minimum of 8M free disk space (10M is recommended) to run in 386 Enhanced mode with all components installed. To run in Standard mode, 6M of free disk space (9M is recommended) is required to install all components. You can reduce the required disk space by eliminating components during installation.

■ At least one floppy disk drive or a CD-ROM drive to install the CD-ROM version.

■ MS-DOS 3.3 or higher. Version 6.0 is recommended.

Optional equipment that Windows supports includes the following:

■ Microsoft or compatible mouse, which is highly recommended.

■ Class 1, Class 2, or Communications Application Specification (CAS) fax modem or network access to one. A Class 1 fax modem is required for binary file transfers.

■ One or more printers or plotters; Windows supports over 250 printers.

■ Hayes or compatible modem.

■ Audio board.

■ CD-ROM drive.

■ Network hardware including cables and a Microsoft-compatible network adapter card.

Before you install Windows 3.11, you need to make sure that you have enough storage available on the hard disk on which you are installing Windows. Type **dir** at the DOS prompt to find the available storage.

Note: *You can install Windows on any hard drive; you do not have to install it on drive C.*

Installing Windows

After you make a list of your equipment, you are ready to install Windows. If you are unfamiliar with computers or are upgrading from a previous version of Windows, you should use Express Setup. If you are familiar with computers or need to customize the installation, use Custom Setup.

Preparing for Installation

Before you install Windows, you may want to prepare for the installation by using the following steps. Note, however, that these steps are not mandatory.

1. Protect your original floppy disks from accidental change. On 3 1/2-inch disks, slide open the *write-protect tab* (a square sliding button at the disk's top edge). On 5 1/4-inch disks, put a write-protect tab (an adhesive patch) over the square notch on the disk's edge. Copy the original disks onto backup disks and store the originals at a separate site.

2. Complete the registration forms and mail them back to Microsoft while you are waiting for segments of the installation to complete. Microsoft uses the registrations to send you special offers on related software, send newsletters containing tips, and inform you when updates to Windows are available. You may not get discount pricing on upgrades unless you are registered.

3. At the DOS prompt, such as c:\>, type **chkdsk /f**. If lost clusters are found, respond Yes to collect them and store them. If you have MS-DOS Version 6.2 or later, run SCANDISK instead of CHKDSK.

Caution

Do not run the CHKDSK /F command while Windows is running.

4. Run a disk-defragmenting or disk-optimization program, if you have one, to make Windows run faster. Because Windows frequently reads and writes information to disk as it operates, you want the information stored on your disk as compactly as possible.

5. Before installing Windows, remove any protected-mode memory-management programs, such as QEMM386, 386Max, or Blue Max. You can prevent these types of programs from running by typing **rem** before the DEVICE= line for each program in the CONFIG.SYS file. Save the revised version of CONFIG.SYS as a text file and then restart your computer.

6. If you are upgrading from an existing Windows or Windows for Workgroups installation, copy or back up all files ending in INI or GRP. If the installation doesn't work correctly, you may need to restore these files to return to your existing installation.

Starting Windows Setup

To install Windows, follow these steps:

1. Start your computer and, if necessary, return to a DOS prompt, such as C:\>.

2. Put Disk 1 in a floppy disk drive and close the door.

3. Type the drive letter, followed by a colon (for example, type **a:** if the disk is in drive A).

4. Press Enter to switch to that disk drive.

5. Type **setup** and press Enter.

The Windows for Workgroups 3.11 welcome screen appears.

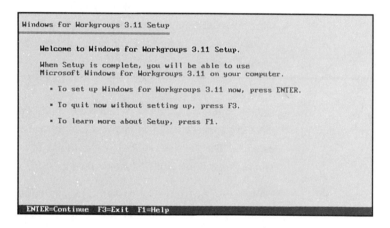

```
Windows for Workgroups 3.11 Setup

   Welcome to Windows for Workgroups 3.11 Setup.

   When Setup is complete, you will be able to use
   Microsoft Windows for Workgroups 3.11 on your computer.

      • To set up Windows for Workgroups 3.11 now, press ENTER.

      • To quit now without setting up, press F3.

      • To learn more about Setup, press F1.




 ENTER=Continue  F3=Exit  F1=Help
```

A

6. Read and follow the directions on-screen. Insert additional floppy disks as you are prompted.

During installation, you are asked where you want to install Windows. The default or automatic choice is

    C:\WINDOWS

You can edit this path name so that Windows is installed on a different hard drive or in a different directory. To edit the path name, use the Backspace key to delete the unnecessary text, and then type the new text. For example, to install Windows on drive D in the directory WIN311, backspace over C:\WINDOWS and type **d:\win311**.

Upgrading an older version of Windows preserves Windows settings, updates printer drivers when necessary, and preserves drivers not recognized by the newer version.

During the installation, you are prompted to enter your name and company name. You *must* enter your name. The program uses it to notify anyone attempting to reinstall the software you have already installed. Press Tab to move between the two edit boxes. Use the arrow keys, Backspace key, or Del key to edit what you type. You are given a chance to make corrections.

If you have problems...   If you have trouble installing Windows because of a terminate-and-stay-resident (TSR) program, exit the installation program, remove the TSR load line from CONFIG.SYS (or add REM to the beginning of the line), and restart your computer so that the TSR does not load. Then restart the Windows installation.

Note: *If you are installing Windows on a network or on a system connected to a network, check with your network administrator for the best method of installing. The file NETWORKS.WRI contains information, in Windows Write format, about installing Windows on a network.*

When you finish installing Windows, a dialog box appears with two buttons: **R**estart Computer and Return to MS-**D**OS. Click either button. The selections you made during Setup do not take effect until you restart your computer by rebooting it. If you chose not to let Setup modify AUTOEXEC.BAT and CONFIG.SYS, Windows may not run correctly, even after you reboot.

Using Express Setup

Express Setup uses settings and hardware configurations that the installation program has determined will run on your system. If you need to, you can change these settings and installation configurations later (see the section "Changing the Setup after Installation" later in this appendix). Here are some of the things Express Setup does:

- Modifies the AUTOEXEC.BAT and CONFIG.SYS files automatically. The old files are saved with new names. Note the new names and consider copying the files to a floppy disk for later use.

■ Searches your hard disks for programs and creates icons and group windows for Windows programs as well as many DOS programs

■ Provides an optional, short tutorial on using a mouse and Windows

Note: *In most cases, you should use Express Setup. If Express Setup does not work correctly, you can install or reinstall other items or features of Windows at a later time by rerunning Setup.*

Using Custom Setup

Custom Setup enables you to specify how you want to install Windows. You can see or select changes as they are made; for example, Express Setup changes the AUTOEXEC.BAT and CONFIG.SYS files automatically, whereas Custom Setup enables you to change those files yourself. Using Custom Setup, you can cross-check the installation process or select hardware configurations different from those automatically selected. Note some of the things Custom Setup does:

■ Displays a list of the hardware it detects. You can accept or change the detected hardware. This option is useful if the type of mouse or video adapter has been incorrectly detected.

You can select a different configuration from the one Windows has detected.

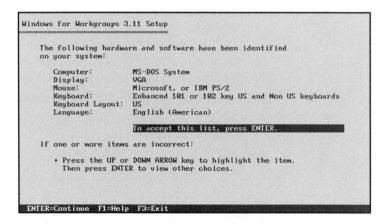

```
Windows for Workgroups 3.11 Setup

    The following hardware and software have been identified
    on your system:

        Computer:           MS-DOS System
        Display:            VGA
        Mouse:              Microsoft, or IBM PS/2
        Keyboard:           Enhanced 101 or 102 key US and Non US keyboards
        Keyboard Layout:    US
        Language:           English (American)

                            To accept this list, press ENTER.

    If one or more items are incorrect:

        • Press the UP or DOWN ARROW key to highlight the item.
          Then press ENTER to view other choices.


ENTER=Continue  F1=Help  F3=Exit
```

■ Displays the changes that Custom Setup will make to AUTOEXEC.BAT and CONFIG.SYS, enabling you to edit the changes. You have the option to accept the modifications, reject them, or make manual changes.

■ Enables you to select the Windows components (such as games and screen savers) and accessory programs that you want to install or don't want to install.

If disk space is limited, you can choose to install only the necessary components.

■ Enables you to select the Windows and DOS programs you want set up automatically within Windows.

■ Gives you the opportunity to take a short tutorial on the mouse and Windows.

In Custom Setup, you make selections in dialog boxes that appear in Windows screens. If you are familiar with Windows operations, use normal Windows selection techniques with the keyboard or mouse. In some Setup dialog boxes, you see a group of boxes with an X beside one of them; that box is selected. To select one of the options, click the box; to deselect the option, click the box again.

Windows also asks whether it can make changes to the AUTOEXEC.BAT and CONFIG.SYS files. The Setup program provides the changes that Windows needs in order to run your computer. You are given three choices for these files:

■ You can accept all changes. Copies of the old files are saved to backup files.

■ You can modify changes. A dialog box displays the original and proposed files. Use the Tab key to move into the top list and edit the proposed changes. You can move around in the proposed text by pressing the arrow keys, delete text by pressing Backspace or Del, and add new text by typing at the insertion point.

■ You can make the changes yourself later.

Installing Printers

You are given a chance to install Windows printer drivers, which tell Windows how to interact with printers. You do not have to install printer drivers at this point, although it is a convenient time. You can install drivers later, using Print Manager, as described in Lesson 6, "Controlling Printers and Fonts."

From the list of printers on-screen, select the names that most closely match your equipment; then choose **I**nstall. Choose Specify **P**ort or **C**onnect to connect your printer to the port where it is physically attached. Choose **S**etup to change paper orientation (vertical or horizontal printing), paper size, number of copies, font cartridges, and so on. Choose Se**t** as Default Printer if you want this printer to be the one on which Windows always proposes to print. You can change these settings later from a program's Printer Setup command or from Windows' Control Panel.

You can install additional printers after installation with the Printers program in Control Panel.

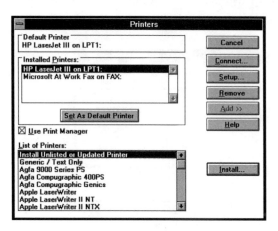

Note: *Each printer has different setup options, and if your printer includes a memory option, be sure to specify how much memory your printer has. (The HP LaserJet III, for example, includes a memory option.)*

A

Installing a Generic Printer Driver

If you cannot locate a printer driver from your printer's manufacturer, Windows offers a temporary solution. One of the choices for a printer driver is Generic/Text Only. Using this choice enables you to print text and numbers on most printers; however, you will not be able to print with special capabilities, such as underline, bold, or graphics.

Contact Microsoft or your printer manufacturer for a driver for your printer or for the name of a compatible driver. Windows supports hundreds of printer drivers. Microsoft maintains a Windows Driver Library (WDL) that contains device drivers supported by Windows 3.11. You can obtain a copy of this library through Microsoft forums on CompuServe, GEnie, America ON-Line, or some public bulletin boards. You can receive a driver also by calling Microsoft.

When you receive a printer driver to match your equipment, you can install the driver without reinstalling Windows. Use Control Panel to add the new printer driver. Consult the documentation shipped with the new driver for information on installation.

Setting Up Applications

During Custom Setup, you can choose to have Windows Setup search for installed programs. Express Setup performs the search automatically.

You can specify the system path or a hard disk to search for installed applications.

If Setup encounters a program file and it cannot identify the program, you are prompted to select the program from a list.

When the search is complete, a list of installed applications is displayed, and you can select the applications for which you want Windows to create program icons and group windows. See Lesson 3, "Working with Groups and Applications," for more information on icons and group windows.

Select one or more applications and then click **A**dd to have Windows set up the applications in Program Manager.

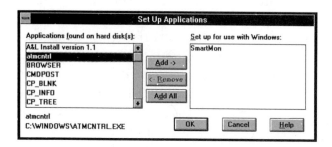

Reviewing Additional Windows Files

At the end of the Windows installation, you are given an opportunity to read the files that Setup copied into the Windows directory. You can read the files from the installation program when it asks you to, or you can complete the installation of Windows and open the files with Write, a word processing program that comes with Windows. The Setup files are described in the following table:

Setup File	Contents
README.WRI	Current updates to the user manual
PRINTERS.WRI	Additional information about configuring printers and fonts
NETWORKS.WRI	Information about installing Windows on networks
MAIL.WRI	Information about using the Mail system
SYSINI.WRI	Information about modifying the SYSTEM.INI file
WININI.WRI	Information about modifying the WIN.INI file

A

Changing the Setup after Installation

After Windows is operating correctly, you can modify its setup without reinstalling the entire Windows system. You may occasionally need to change your configuration. For example, you may have a portable computer running Windows. When you are on the road, you will need to use the portable's plasma or LCD screen, but when you are at the office, you will want to use a high-resolution color monitor. Instead of reinstalling Windows to get the new video driver, you can use the Windows Setup program to switch between the drivers you will be using. Windows Setup is also useful when you buy and attach a new keyboard or mouse, or when you attach your computer to a network.

The Windows Setup program is located in the Main group window of Program Manager. To change the setup of the display, keyboard, or mouse after Windows is installed, follow these steps:

1. Click the Windows Setup program icon in the Main group window.

The Windows Setup dialog box appears.

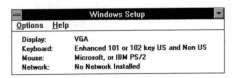

2. From the Windows Setup dialog box, pull down the **O**ptions menu and choose the **C**hange System Settings command.

From the Change System Settings dialog box, you can change installation settings for **D**isplay, **K**eyboard, and **M**ouse.

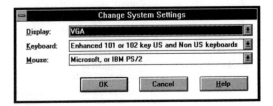

3. To see the pull-down list for the setting you want to change, click the underlined arrow beside the appropriate list box.

4. From the pull-down list, select the type of device you want to install.

5. Choose OK.

6. If a special driver is required, you may be prompted to insert one of the original Windows disks or a disk from the manufacturer of your monitor, keyboard, or mouse.

7. After you create the new setup, you must restart Windows. You are given the choice of restarting Windows or returning to DOS. If you need to change hardware—such as attaching a new keyboard or mouse, or connecting a new monitor—return to DOS, make the new connection, and then restart Windows.

If you have problems...	If Windows or a Windows program does not "behave" correctly after you change the setup, check the Windows Setup dialog box to see whether you have the correct settings. If necessary, return to the original settings or reinstall Windows.
	If you changed the monitor setting and your screen goes black after restarting Windows, the new setting is incorrect. Change to the Windows directory (usually C:\WINDOWS) and type **setup** at the DOS prompt. The Setup screen appears, listing the current selections for hardware. Change the Display setting to match your monitor, press Enter to exit the screen, and restart Windows.

A

Starting and Logging In to Windows for Workgroups

When you start Windows 3.11 for Workgroups, the logon dialog box appears. The **L**ogon Name has been entered for you; this name matches your user name on the network. You can use this name or type a new one. If you share your computer with coworkers, each person should have a unique logon name.

You must also enter your password to access the network. The password is assigned by your network administrator.

You must log on to the network when you start Windows for Workgroups.

Note: *If you have any questions about your logon name or password, ask your network administrator.*

Appendix B

Optimizing Windows 3.11

This appendix shows you how to make adjustments on your system and in your working habits to increase the efficiency of Windows. The following list of suggestions covers a wide range of topics. Additional information on optimizing Windows (with and without a network) can be found in Que's *Tuning Windows 3.1* and *Using Windows*, 3.11 Edition, Special Edition. Information on working with Windows or Windows for Workgroups on a Novell network can be found in Que's *Using NetWare 3.12*, Special Edition.

Note: *If you are running on a network, consult your system administrator before making any changes to your system.*

Here are some suggestions for optimizing Windows 3.11:

- Consider your hardware capabilities when running Windows. If you have a 386 system with only two or three megabytes of memory, Windows performance will degrade rapidly if you try to run more than one application at a time. If you have a 486 system with 16 megabytes of memory, you should be able to run as many applications as you want without degrading Windows performance.

- Assess your current memory configuration and consider purchasing additional memory for your system. Additional memory will significantly improve Windows performance, so add as much as you can afford. This is one of the most important changes you can make to improve Windows performance.

- Limit your use of graphic features in Windows programs. For example, turn off toolbars, rulers, and ribbons if you don't need them. These features make it easier for you to work in an application, but they can diminish the application's performance.

■ Use a Draft viewing mode if available in the application. Graphic display options show you the document as it will appear when printed, which is convenient. These options, however, take up huge amounts of memory and can drastically affect system performance.

■ When printing, choose a printer font (marked in the list with a printer icon) rather than a TrueType font (marked with a TT icon) to decrease the time it takes to print.

■ If you are on a network, configure Print Manager to print directly to the network port. You can still use Print Manager to manage printers and print queues, but you eliminate the Print Manager queue from the process.

■ Open the Fonts program in Control Panel and remove any fonts you don't use. This will speed up the time it takes to load Windows and Windows applications that use those fonts.

■ Reduce the number of applications in your StartUp group. With too many applications in that group, you can run out of system re-sources before all the applications are loaded, and it takes Windows longer to start.

■ Consider limiting the number of open group windows in Program Manager to speed up loading Windows.

■ Many Windows applications support multiple document windows. However, the more documents you have open, the slower your system will run. Larger documents also slow down performance.

■ Reduce the number of TSR (terminate-and-stay-resident) programs you run on your system. These programs take up memory and slow down the system.

■ If you have a monitor configured to run in SVGA (640x800) or 8514/a (1024x768) mode, consider reconfiguring to VGA (640x480) mode. If your monitor is set up for 16 million colors, consider cutting back to 256 or even 16 colors. These changes will substantially increase video performance, which is a significant factor in Windows programs.

■ Increase the efficiency of your hard drive by running a disk-defragmentation program, such as DOS 6.2's DEFRAG or Norton Utilities' Speed Disk. These programs should never be used while Windows is running or on a compressed drive.

■ Create a permanent swap file on your system. Give the swap file as much disk space as you can afford, allowing enough disk space for temporary files. The temporary files created when printing large documents can require several megabytes of disk space. It's a good idea to run a defragmentation program before creating the swap file.

■ Install the latest version of DOS. MS-DOS 6.0 (and later) includes the MEMMAKER program, which automatically configures your AUTOEXEC.BAT and CONFIG.SYS files to maximize system performance.

■ Increase the amount of available disk space by deleting or archiving unnecessary files (copy them to a floppy disk and then delete the original files).

■ Regularly delete the temporary files created by Windows. It's a good idea to create a directory just for your temporary files so that they are easy to find. You will need to add a command to your AUTOEXEC.BAT file telling Windows the name of the directory where you want your temporary files stored (such as SET TEMP=C:\TEMP). The drive you use for temporary files should have plenty of space and should not be a network drive. Also make sure that you exit Windows before you delete temporary files.

■ Run the CHKDSK /F command (or the SCANDISK command if you have DOS 6.2 or later) to find and repair problems on the disk. If you are running the CHKDSK command, always answer Yes to the question to repair lost chains. Utility programs, such as Norton Utilities, are also available to diagnose and repair problems with drives.

B

Index

C

Q-R

Windows QuickStart, 3.11 Edition, *DiskPack* Order Form

Use this form to order the *Windows QuickStart*, 3.11 Edition, *DiskPack*. It contains approximately 30 pages of additional exercises that build on the examples presented in the lessons. These "hands on" exercises enable you to further your learning of Windows by practicing with sample files (rather than creating new files or working with important Windows or application files). The *DiskPack* includes a 720K DD 3 1/2-inch disk that contains practice files for use with these exercises.

The easiest way to order your *Windows QuickStart*, 3.11 Edition, *DiskPack* is to pick up the phone and call

1-800-428-5331

between 9:00 a.m. and 5:00 p.m. EST.

For faster service, please have your credit card available.

ISBN	Quantity	Item	Unit Cost	Total Cost
1-56529-865-9D		*Windows QuickStart, 3.11 Edition, DiskPack*	$7.99*	

*The unit price includes the shipping and handling charges for domestic orders. For overseas shipping and handling, add $2.00 per DiskPack. Price subject to change.

If you need it NOW, we can ship it to you so that you will receive the *DiskPack* overnight or in two days for an additional charge of approximately $18.00.

Que Corporation
201 W. 103rd Street
Indianapolis, Indiana 46290

Orders: 1-800-428-5331
Sales Fax: 1-800-448-3804
Customer Service Fax: 1-800-835-3202

GO AHEAD. PLUG YOURSELF INTO
MACMILLAN COMPUTER PUBLISHING.

Introducing the Macmillan Computer Publishing Forum on CompuServe®

Yes, it's true. Now, you can have CompuServe access to the same professional, friendly folks who have made computers easier for years. On the Macmillan Computer Publishing Forum, you'll find additional information on the topics covered by every Macmillan Computer Publishing imprint—including Que, Sams Publishing, New Riders Publishing, Alpha Books, Brady Books, Hayden Books, and Adobe Press. In addition, you'll be able to receive technical support and disk updates for the software produced by Que Software and Paramount Interactive, a division of the Paramount Technology Group. It's a great way to supplement the best information in the business.

WHAT CAN YOU DO ON THE MACMILLAN COMPUTER PUBLISHING FORUM?

Play an important role in the publishing process—and make our books better while you make your work easier:

- Leave messages and ask questions about Macmillan Computer Publishing books and software—you're guaranteed a response within 24 hours
- Download helpful tips and software to help you get the most out of your computer
- Contact authors of your favorite Macmillan Computer Publishing books through electronic mail
- Present your own book ideas
- Keep up to date on all the latest books available from each of Macmillan Computer Publishing's exciting imprints

JOIN NOW AND GET A FREE COMPUSERVE STARTER KIT!

To receive your free CompuServe Introductory Membership, call toll-free, **1-800-848-8199** and ask for representative **#597**. The Starter Kit Includes:

- Personal ID number and password
- $15 credit on the system
- Subscription to CompuServe Magazine

HERE'S HOW TO PLUG INTO MACMILLAN COMPUTER PUBLISHING:

Once on the CompuServe System, type any of these phrases to access the Macmillan Computer Publishing Forum:

GO MACMILLAN   **GO BRADY**
GO QUEBOOKS   **GO HAYDEN**
GO SAMS   **GO QUESOFT**
GO NEWRIDERS   **GO ALPHA**

Once you're on the CompuServe Information Service, be sure to take advantage of all of CompuServe's resources. CompuServe is home to more than 1,700 products and services—plus it has over 1.5 million members worldwide. You'll find valuable online reference materials, travel and investor services, electronic mail, weather updates, leisure-time games and hassle-free shopping (no jam-packed parking lots or crowded stores).

Seek out the hundreds of other forums that populate CompuServe. Covering diverse topics such as pet care, rock music, cooking, and political issues, you're sure to find others with the same concerns as you—and expand your knowledge at the same time.